TEACHER ASSEMBLAGE

Teacher Assemblage

By

Taylor Webb
University of British Columbia, Canada

SENSE PUBLISHERS
ROTTERDAM / TAIPEI

A C.I.P. record for this book is available from the Library of Congress.

ISBN 978-90-8790-778-5 (paperback)
ISBN 978-90-8790-779-2 (hardback)
ISBN 978-90-8790-780-8 (e-book)

Published by: Sense Publishers,
P.O. Box 21858, 3001 AW Rotterdam, The Netherlands
http://www.sensepublishers.com

Printed on acid-free paper

From my father, to my son.

TABLE OF CONTENTS

A COMMENT ON METHOD

There are teaching holograms in England.[1] They are not teachers. They look like teachers; they act like teachers; they talk like teachers. In many ways the holograms resemble teachers. But they are not teachers. The holograms are transmitted into mathematics classrooms. They dispense information. Holograms are able to circumvent the spatial limitations of schools and the spatial limitations of geography across districts. They are spatially efficient. Holograms also reduce costs associated with corporeal teachers. Holograms replace teachers. Hence, holograms are economically efficient. Curiously, this technology, intended to replace teachers, also resembles them. However, this is not a teacher.

THE TREACHERY OF IMAGES

In 1929 René Magritte created a painting titled *The Treachery of Images (This Is Not a Pipe)*. Magritte's painting renders an ordinary tobacco pipe. Just below the image, Magritte painted the words "Ceci n'est pas une pipe" (This is not a pipe). The painting challenged audiences to make sense of an apparent contradiction. One might ask, for instance, if not a pipe, then what? The straightforward answer to the conundrum elicited by Magritte is the affirmative – that is, of course this is not a pipe, it is a rendering of a pipe. Such a simple answer, while correct, circumvents a more fundamental question asked by Magritte: What constitutes identity?

Magritte often painted ordinary objects in his work, and he was able to give new life to objects by representing them in strange ways and odd contexts. Magritte's paintings were simultaneously familiar and strange, immediately understood and immediately perplexing. Magritte commented frequently on the fact that identity was located in different spatial arrangements and that identity was produced over time and through a politics of space. In this way, Magritte expressed the many ways that identity was mutable and that contexts were malleable. This is also a way to describe teachers in the twenty-first century.

By extension, what is the relationship between the hologram and its referent, the teacher? What criteria constitute something as "real" and something as represented? Do teachers possess a fixed corporeal identity, and is this identity necessary for the pedagogical process? What effects will *imaging* have on teachers and teaching? Do teachers auto-represent, or self-represent, themselves and their pedagogy? How? Why?

Figure 1. René Magritte. The Treachery of Images (This Is Not a Pipe). (1926). © Estate of
René Magritte / SODRAC (2008)

This book documents how teachers image themselves in attempts to mediate
educational conflicts in schools. It explores the costs associated with imaging
pedagogy. Why represent pedagogy? What does it look like? How are
representations of pedagogy created? What effects are produced in the subjectivity
of teachers who self-image? Can the process of self-representation be controlled?

THIS IS NOT A BOOK

By introducing the book this way, my intent was twofold. First, I have introduced
the book in broad strokes, introduced the kinds of issues that it will examine, and
introduced how I discuss the strange realities of pedagogical self-representation. I
use surrealist art throughout to explain the strange realities teachers inhabit and
produce. Surrealist art often destabilizes what is taken for granted and provides
powerful visual anecdotes about ideas of desire, subjectivity, and the unconscious.
Surrealist art provides pointed commentary on what might be called a modernist
way of thinking. Teachers, I will argue, work within the temporal distortions that
exist between the modern and postmodern epochs of education.

Second, I introduce the book this way to describe the method used to narrate its
story. This study is supported by my readings of both Michel Foucault and Gilles
Deleuze. Both Foucault and Deleuze were influenced by surrealism. In fact, it is
impossible to read Foucault and Deleuze and not run into surrealist artists like

Marcel Duchamp, Salvador Dali, Antonin Artaud, Georges Bataille, and Henry Miller, to name but a few.[2]

Foucault and René Magritte were acquaintances and exchanged written correspondence in which they discussed their respective work. Foucault (1970) borrowed the title for one of his books – *The Order of Things* – from the title of one of Magritte's art exhibitions in New York City. Later, Foucault (1983c) would write a small book about the ways identity can be represented and ultimately changed through repeated representations. Foucault (1983c) used Magritte's painting – *This Is Not a Pipe* – as the foil of his text. In that text, Foucault (1983c) observed, "A day will come when, by means of similitude relayed indefinitely along the length of a series, the image itself, along with the name it bears, will lose its identity" (p. 54). In this book, I will argue with regard to teachers and teaching that that day is today.

NOTES

[1] http://news.bbc.co.uk/2/hi/in_depth/education/2000/bett2000/600667.stm

[2] I am less interested in the particular departure points of surrealism that Foucault and Deleuze used in their thinking. Such a project might be loosely considered a genealogy into surrealism and its influence on continental philosophy. Such a project would produce an entirely different project than the current one. My use of surrealist art attempts to represent visually some of the changes in teachers' realities and to simultaneously identify some of the influences of Michel Foucault and Gilles Deleuze. Again, my goal of examining teachers' fabrications is to also provide a richer understanding of the theories used to support this study.

ACKNOWLEDGEMENTS

I wish to thank Ken Sirotnik who saw something in this work when others didn't. I am grateful to Peter de Liefde for his patience through the preparation process.

Many thanks are due to Paul Loeb for sustaining a conversation with me about Michel Foucault and Gilles Deleuze for nearly twenty years. Those conversations have been some of the most memorable moments of my life. I am grateful Christopher John Lewis for another set of conversations about "lived aesthetics" and our own "arts of living." I have always been inspired by his work and will always remember our nomadic wanderings.

I wish to thank Lesley Erickson for her keen eye. Her editing services were excellent. I am also indebted to Sarah Lapierre at the Society for Reproduction Rights of Authors, Composers and Publishers in Canada (SODRAC). Sarah's assistance helped me write the book that I had envisioned.

Finally, and most importantly, I thank Amy Rudzinski and Owen. You both are what make living these arts so worthwhile.

I acknowledge with much gratitude the following publishing sources for the material used throughout the book. I appreciate their permission to modify and reprint those excerpts into the book.

Webb, P. T. (2008). Re-mapping power in educational micropolitics. *Critical Studies in Education, 49*(2), 127-142.

Webb, P. T. (2007). Accounting for teacher knowledge: Reterritorializations as epistemic suicide. *Discourse: Studies in the Cultural Politics of Education, 29*(3), 279-295.

Webb, P. T. (2006). The choreography of accountability. *Journal of Education Policy, 21*(2), 201-214.

Webb, P. T. (2005). The anatomy of accountability. *Journal of Education Policy, 20*(2), 189-208.

Webb, P. T. (2002). Teacher power: The exercise of professional autonomy in an era of strict accountability. *Teacher Development, 6*(1), 47-61.

CHAPTER 1

TERRITORIALIZING WARS OVER TEACHERS' KNOWLEDGE

The Pleasures of Micropolitical Resistance

Schools are political environments, and teachers exercise considerable power regarding policy outcomes. External policies produce a maelstrom of micropolitical activity when definitions of teaching and learning are contested among teachers, parents, administrators, and state bureaucrats. Schools, consequently, are places of conflict where competing (and often incompatible) interests and understandings about education are negotiated.

One way to control teachers is to keep them ignorant about their power. Ineffective teacher preparation that ignores questions about power, for instance, is akin to keeping teachers in a cave (Plato, 2006). Another way to control teachers is to develop accountability schemes, including schemes to intimidate teachers for particular policy outcomes, that direct this power. As a result, teachers can be co-opted for political desires that have nothing to do with children, youth, or humanity (Fenstermacher & Amarel, 1983).

However, Maxcy (1991) argued that teachers should control their work by using a type of normative power:

> Professionalism implies a kind of normative power. Educational professionals ought to have the power to form directives for action with regard to problems arising out of the exercise of their skills and expertise. Teaching professionals ought to have the power to make policy and policy decisions. By professionalism, I have in mind power being placed in the hands of educators such that they may possess leadership in policy and decision making affecting learning in schools. (p. 160)

Should teachers control the policy environments of schools? What are the criteria for the responsible use of teacher power? The answers to these kinds of questions rest upon understanding how power operates in education.

Lortie (1975) recognized the problem of teachers and power 30 years ago. He suggested that "important research could be done on the issue of power and teachers" (p. 102). Lortie observed that questions about teachers' professional identity surfaced once discussions moved away from *what* should be taught (curricula) and *how* it should be taught (pedagogy) to discussions about *who* should make educational decisions. Moreover, Lortie documented how teachers found pleasure in directing the implementation of curricular and assessment policies in schools. Lortie stated that "teacher power [was traditionally] limited to specified authority over students; teachers were not supposed to *enjoy* exercising power [over, or through policy]" (p. 102, italics in original).

I conducted this study because I wanted to add empirical evidence to debates about how teachers exercise power in schools. I agreed with Sirotnik (1989) when he stated, "It must not be forgotten where the ultimate power to change is and always has been – in the heads, hands, and hearts of the educators who work in our schools" (p. 109). I am interested in the nature of this power. How does it operate? Toward what goals? On what basis? What is desirable about teaching, and how is exercising power in schools pleasurable? Are there illusions about the use of power that perpetuates how power uses teachers?

I hoped to understand how teachers interacted with power as a way to negotiate the political nature of their work. That is, I was interested in teachers' micropolitics, in their power. I was also interested in the effect power had on teachers.

PROFESSIONAL IDENTITIES AND DESIRING SUBJECTIVITIES

In this chapter I introduce how the problem of teacher power is rooted in historical tensions about teachers' professional identity. On the one hand, teachers' professional identity pivots on competing ideas about what their roles in the classroom should be and the kinds of knowledge they should have. Stated simply, some administrators and scholars believe that teachers should follow knowledge developed by others, while others believe that teachers should lead policy development based on an exclusive, or professional, knowledge base (Maxcy, 1991).

On the other hand, the idea of an endemic knowledge base for teachers has been increasingly disqualified. Specifically, the professional-identity discourse surrounding teachers is antiquated and reflects transnational attempts to control education for economic and labor purposes. If democratic education is even necessary – so goes the argument – it is only in relation to the economic, technological, and military needs of the twenty-first century. As many governments have stated, the stakes for state capital are too high to allow teachers to define what counts in education. In fact, governments are more interested in leveraging their control over teachers to maximize economic returns for nation-states than they are in connecting education to its rightful place in the larger democratic project (see, for instance, Psacharopoulos & Patrinos, 2004). And, as I will demonstrate, teachers incur psychic costs when they engage in micropolitics for democratic purposes. These psychic costs are too high when corporate states maintain a perspective that teachers simply represent "human capital stock" that is easily replaced (OECD, 2007, p. 26).

Evidence about what teachers have become has followed debates about the professional identity of teachers. Accountability policies have severely curtailed teacher power in the normative sense. The notion of a professional identity – core self, unique individual, professional autonomy, professional knowledge – is an idea that has slowly been disqualified as evidence of teachers' multiple identities has surfaced. Teachers have developed bifurcated identities as accountability policies have transmogrified their normative power into forms of state capital and utility.[1] Nevertheless, questions about teachers' normative power persist – either in (1) the production of spaces that assist teachers to resist macropolitical desires or (2) the assembling of teachers' subjectivities into additional monitors for government control.

Chapter Organization

This chapter is organized into three sections. First, I discuss how scholars have tried to create a knowledge base as a strategy to professionalize teaching. I demonstrate how the idea of teachers' knowledge is, at best, a vigorous debate within the scholarship on teaching. I argue that this debate has produced a knowledge crisis for and *in* teachers.

The second section presents the argument that the corporate state has interceded in this fractured epistemic territory. Governments now understand themselves as institutions that clean up the failures of teacher education through "soft" and "hard" forms of accountability. I examine how curricular policy has controlled teachers' fractured knowledge and, in this sense, how curricular policy has acted as a soft form of teacher accountability (often through the guise of professional development). Evidence that teacher micropolitics have emerged within attempts to develop soft forms of accountability is important to this discussion. In these instances, teachers' bifurcated identities surfaced when they enjoyed instructional problem solving that simultaneously resisted disingenuous attempts at school reform. I discuss this "schizophrenia" as the birth of the micropolitical pedagogue.

The third and final section examines the contemporary hard form of educational accountability. Once corporate states recognized how to harness teacher power through curricular policy, they noted the enormous economic, technological, and military benefits that could be accrued by controlling teachers' cognitions. Unlike soft forms of accountability, hard forms were designed to colonize teachers' souls, epistemologies, and subjectivities (Ball, 2003; Zembylas, 2003).

TERRITORIALIZING TEACHERS' KNOWLEDGE: A STRATEGY TO PROFESSIONALIZE TEACHING

Teaching has been marked by an aura of conservatism that has been impervious to change since the mid-1960s (Lortie, 1975). This conservatism is rooted in debates about the nature of teachers' knowledge and their roles in using this knowledge. On one side of these debates, people have argued that teaching is simply a matter of having a "firm grasp of subject matter and basic skill," and that teacher professionalization models are "precisely the wrong direction" in which to move in order to improve education (MacDonald, 1998). These viewpoints on teaching have often been called "technical" because they prescribe what teachers should know and be able to do.

Much of the technical perspective of teaching stems from the "process-product" research of the late 1960s and early 1970s. This research looked for causal links between teacher effectiveness and particular teaching practices. For instance, the Florida Performance Measurement System is an observation instrument that identifies teachers' strengths and weaknesses according to items coded for specific teacher behaviors. Items such as "begins instruction promptly," "orients/maintains focus," "provides for practice" are easily observable behaviors and, when demonstrated by teachers, generate a purportedly "successful" teaching episode. Failure to execute a percentage of behaviors generates a purportedly "poor" teaching episode. In extreme cases, teachers are removed entirely from the process of student learning, as is illustrated by cases of "teacher-proof" curricula and certain digital technologies. It is believed that teachers impede learning because they act as inefficient middle managers during the transmission of subject matter to students.

Unfortunately, the process-product research reified teachers' low status through at least two faulty assumptions about how students learn. First, students are not passive receivers of teaching treatments. Looking for one-way causal links between predetermined categories overlooks the fact that students are implicated in the learning process (Vygotsky, 1962). Second, much of this research based its idea of effectiveness on students' test scores. Test scores, by themselves, are too narrowly defined to account for student learning and, thus, do not provide accurate descriptions of what students have learned (Kennedy, 1999).

Teacher Professionalism

There are three generally accepted ideas about what constitutes a professional in the educational literature (Timperley & Alton-Lee, 2008). First, a professional must possess a large degree of talent and skill. Second, professionals must use a body of knowledge that supports their work. And third, professionals must have the autonomy to make decisions that marry skills with knowledge to solve complex problems. Proponents of these conceptual arguments insist that teachers need to engage in complex thinking to be effective in their jobs. These arguments are based on the idea that teaching is far more complex than any list of predetermined categories could hope to capture.

Firstly, teaching categories do not account for the sophisticated content that needs to be taught to a variety of learners (Segall, 2004). There is simply too much subject matter complexity and student variability to use static teaching techniques. Secondly, the reduction of teaching to a set of techniques narrows the act of learning to acquiring a set of behaviors. Learning is much more than acquiring new behaviors (Vygotsky, 1962). Thirdly, teaching is a moral endeavor wherein teachers make frequent decisions about complex ethical issues (Ayers, 2004). Teachers who rely on teaching techniques that fail to consider the moral implications of their role in the classroom neglect the public mission of educating competent and caring citizens in a democracy. And, fourthly, teaching is essentially a political act (Costigan, Zumwalt, & Crocco, 2004). Failure to prepare teachers for democratic engagement is professionally irresponsible (Oakes & Lipton, 2002).

In the last three decades, studies have attempted to describe teachers' knowledge and cognition. Shulman (1986) argued that teachers make complex decisions about how best to combine teaching skills with subject matter depending on different students' needs and classroom situations. This professional premise ushered in a research area that sought to create a teaching profession.

Territorializing Teacher Knowledge: Provinces and Landscapes

For nearly 30 years scholars have debated the source of teacher knowledge and the kinds of cognitive processes associated with such knowledge (Clandinin & Connelly, 1996; Cochran-Smith & Lytle, 1999; Elbaz, 1981; Putnam & Borko, 2000; Shulman, 1986). The debate pivots on whether and the extent to which teacher knowledge is an endemic form of knowledge – often referred to as practical, craft, situational, event-structured, episodic, context-determined, or context-dependent (Carter, 1990; Elbaz, 1983) – and the extent to which teacher knowledge can be codified and generalized (Grossman, 1989; Wilson & Wineburg, 1993; Shulman, 1986). Nowhere is this debate more evident than in exchanges between Diorio (1982), Tom (1983) and Elbaz and Elbaz (1983).

I identify epistemic fissures within each paradigm that result from inadequate accounts of power, and I describe teachers' schizophrenia as the result of these bifurcated attempts at identity development. In the end, I argue that any conception of teacher knowledge must answer questions about teachers' power within professionalization attempts.

Codifiable and generalizable knowledge
The debate over teacher knowledge is motivated, minimally, by preferences about the kinds of activities teachers ought to experience when learning to teach. The codifiable paradigm assumed that teacher knowledge was propositional and theoretical; thus, teacher learning occurred with knowledge transfer (of instruction, of curricula, etc.) and, subsequently, through knowledge application (in the field, in the laboratory, etc.). Shulman (1986) coined the phrase "pedagogical content knowledge" as an endemic territory or, in his words, a "unique province" within his larger framework of teacher knowledge. The idea of pedagogical content knowledge was Shulman's (1986) attempt to territorialize teachers' knowledge for purposes of professionalization. Challenges to the codifiable paradigm stemmed from problems of theory and practice as teachers wrestled with applying propositional knowledge to a multitude of contexts, indeed, for some scholars, to contexts of infinite complexity.

A limitation nested in the codifiable paradigm is the extent to which the paradigm recognized the political contexts in which teacher knowledge is developed, practiced, and contested. Gutmann (1999) argued that professionalization attempts that failed to identify power boundaries provided an entrée for nearly any macropolitical group to claim educational and pedagogical sovereignty. Examples of strategies to minimize so-called contextual complications included pedagogical "tool kits" or "teacher-proof" curricula extrapolated from pedagogical propositions. In certain codifiable systems, teacher cognition was removed entirely, creating pedagogical technocrats who transmit corporate, government, and religious interests via the school curriculum. And perhaps in the penultimate achievement of educator skepticism and scorn, the holographic teacher was developed on principles of propositional knowledge.[2]

Event-structured and personal knowledge
Connelly and Clandinin (1995) described the situational view of teacher knowledge as personal and narrative in form. In this view, a teacher's personal-practical knowledge was implicated within any conceptualization of their work and accounted for much of their actions. That is, teachers created knowledge instead of simply consuming it. Clandinin (1992) suggested that teacher knowledge "is a kind of knowledge, carved out of, and shaped by, situations; knowledge that is constructed and reconstructed as they live out their stories and retell and relive them through the process of reflection" (p. 125). Teacher knowledge was affected by, and through, the contexts in which such knowledge was situated – knowledge *in situ*. Clandinin and Connelly (1995) coined the metaphor "professional knowledge landscape" to map the cognitive geographies and territorial borders of teacher knowledge:

> A landscape metaphor allows us to talk about space, place, and time. Furthermore, it has a sense of expansiveness and the possibility of being filled with diverse people, things, and events in different relationships ... Because we see the professional knowledge landscape as composed of relationships among people, places, and things, we see it as both an intellectual and moral landscape. (p. 5)

The landscape metaphor described teaching as ethical action bound by conflicting contexts of schooling and by teachers' own personal-practical knowledge – a territory assumed to be exclusively theirs. However, a limitation nested within a situational conception of teacher knowledge was the extent to which teachers were aware of power operating *within* their landscapes. For instance, Hyland (2005) demonstrated how unrecognized power elements within knowledge landscapes created situations in which teachers reproduced inequitable schooling practices. Webb (2001) noted how a teacher's own racist biases, paradoxically, often directed attempts at antiracism. Scholars noted, then, that teacher knowledge, by itself, was necessary but insufficient to guide teachers' work because of the probability of perpetuating injustice. Scholars argued that "practical wisdom" and *phronesis* were important forms of knowledge that could be used as signposts or map legends within deterritorialized knowledge borders (Coulter & Wiens, 2002).

Figure 2. Desert landscape. © Julie Rudzinski

DETERRITORIALIZING TEACHERS' KNOWLEDGE: TEACHERS AS NOMADS

For (too) many, the perceived idiosyncrasies associated with teacher knowledge smacks of relativism, subjectivism, a cavalier disregard for "scientific" rigor, and an illegitimate basis for "evidence" in educational research (Feuer, Towne, & Shavelson, 2002). Hence, teacher knowledges were characterized as *absent knowledges* because people perceived little or no consistency among various teacher's thinking. As a result, teachers were portrayed as lacking professional knowledge and, hence, as being unaccountable for their actions, a portrayal that challenged their claims to professional identity (Cochran-Smith & Fries, 2001). At best, teachers' professional identities become schizophrenic, or assembled with multiple identities, as a result of their knowledge exterritorialization (Ball, 2003; Deleuze & Guattari, 1987).[3]

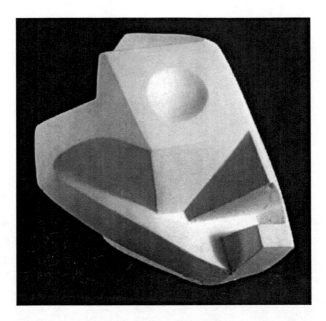

Figure 3. Alberto Giacometti. Head-Skull. (1934). © Estate of Alberto Giacometti /
SODRAC (2008)

Both conceptions of teacher knowledge – codifiable and personal – use spatial metaphors to position teacher identity. Specifically, both conceptions of teacher knowledge link teacher identity to landscapes, territories, or provinces. However, teacher knowledge spaces have become untended or overgrown in the absence of articulations of teacher identity that take into account historical issues of power. Without references to teachers' power, the idyllic landscapes presumed to be the sovereign territories of teachers have been deterritorialized by scholars and by governments: "Deterritorialization is a result of the territory itself being taken as an object, as a material to stratify" (Deleuze & Guattari, 1987, p. 433). A 30-year war over teachers' knowledge has terraformed teachers' cognitive geographies. Teacher knowledge landscapes are now populated with strange creatures, secret gardens, and circular pathways. Artist Max Ernst created several paintings that depicted the less than idyllic representations of landscapes that emerged from the effects of war.[4]

Crucially, the act of terraforming knowledge territories figures teachers as

*Figure 4. Max Ernst. The eye of Silence. 1943-1944. © Estate of Max Ernst /
SODRAC (2008).*

nomads. Teachers wander across desolate territories. Traditional borders of
sovereign epistemes are transformed into political battles for the right to control
teachers' cognitions. Teachers' epistemic land is malleable and provides
opportunities for the new colonization, the next Manifest Destiny, the New World
Order of capitalism and economic production. Deleuze and Guattari (1987)
elaborate:

> Nomads have no points, paths, or land, even though they do by all
> appearances … With the nomad … it is deterritorialization that constitutes
> the relation to earth, to such a degree that the nomad reterritorializes on
> deterritorialization itself. It is the earth that deterritorializes itself, in a way
> that provides the nomad with a territory. The land ceases to be land, tending
> to become simply ground (sol) or support. The earth does not become
> deterritorialized in its global and relative movement, but at specific locations,
> at the spot where the forest recedes, or where the steppe and the desert
> advance. (pp. 381-382)

Again, Max Ernst developed a series of paintings that illustrated the surrealist
transmogrification of "nature," or landscape, into haunting apocalypses that
residents now traverse and from where their work is situated.

9

ACCOUNTING FOR TEACHERS' KNOWLEDGE

Disagreements about who should direct school policy exacerbate teachers' professional schizophrenia through knowledge atrophy. Discussions about accountability, then, are proxies for debates about the control of education. When these discussions are levied against teachers, the discussions attempt to control the production of schooling.

Figure 5. Max Ernst. Europe after the rain. 1940-1942. © Estate of Max Ernst / SODRAC (2008).

The next two sections begin with the assumption that discussions about teacher accountability are about *power* in relation to representative democracies that utilize contested notions of *truth* to guide education policy. To sharpen this assertion, I argue that discussions about teacher accountability rarely occur in totalitarian governments or in pseudodemocratic nations (Zakaria, 1997), where power and truth have been determined a priori – for example, by lineage, military force, or as the result of a theology that omits education in the liberal tradition (i.e., omits education for specific groups, e.g., females). Teachers simply transmit totalitarian ideology explicitly.

A corollary to the above thought is that totalitarian governments often discuss ways to hold indoctrination practices accountable to ideology. This assumption provides a counter-example to forms of teacher accountability that are sought after in representative democracies that hope to ensure something that can be described as educative (i.e., truth, knowledge, rights, equality, progress, emancipation, justice, enlightenment, and so on). It is here that distinctions between education and indoctrination exist. It is also in this political space that governments use various forms of accountability (power) to maintain control. Thus, discussions about holding teachers accountable (e.g., in the pursuit of Western truth) in totalitarian regimes remain largely nonsensical, but discussions about ensuring knowledge indoctrination are completely plausible (and sometimes psychologically and physically painful). Thus, accountability effects are material and real (but the knowledges vary), and the ways these knowledges are held accountable are fluid.

Finally, given that representative democracies have survived through capitalist structures, discussions about holding teachers accountable parallel discussions about disciplining democracies economically. Given this implicit framework, an analysis of teachers' accountability can be pursued. More importantly, this framework identifies forms of indoctrination articulated in capitalist democracies that seek educational knowledges from specific research practices for continued economic production. Consequently, this framework identifies the contemporary (perhaps quintessential) agon about education as a contest between economic production and democratic enlightenment. This agon is irritated when democratic governments control teachers' knowledge and its production through accountability policies.

What remain in representative democracies are political responses to those policies.

THE SOFT ACCOUNTABILITY OF CURRICULAR POLICY AND TEACHERS' MICROPOLITICS

Evidence of how teachers exercise power originated in research on curricular policy implementation. It is here that teachers have most profoundly resisted curricular objectives intended to hold them accountable. In other words, curricular policy conflicts – forms of knowledge control – produce spaces for the micropolitical pedagogue to operate. When policy objectives conflict with what teachers believe – or threaten to remove the enjoyment of their work – the micropolitical game commences. Teachers pursue their nomadic journeys in knowledge landscapes that are constantly reterritorialized, or terraformed, and through which teachers either resist macrodesires and/or compound their cognitive deterritorialization.

The manner in which teachers have exercised power, not simply to resist macropolicy for selfish reasons but also to influence the working conditions of schools in ways they believe will assist students, is central to this discussion. I consider this a legitimate form of microresistance and relate my discussion of it to several research studies that examine teachers' strong motivations to control the teaching and learning practices in classrooms. I use empirical work from micropolitics, policy implementation, and curriculum studies to illustrate these points. I do examine studies to illustrate how teachers' political actions have not been motivated by educational concerns but rather by self-interest. In these studies, the exercise of power is fragmented, confused, and epistemologically suicidal.

Accountability policies in K-12 education therefore both raise questions about who should make educational decisions for students and perpetuate doubts that teachers can or should be responsible (Maxcy, 1991). Difficult questions about student learning pit teachers against curriculum developers, and these conflicts boil down to questions about who has legitimate knowledge about students, teaching, and learning and raise new questions about how this knowledge is legitimated (Pinar et al., 1995). Instead of developing teachers' expertise and knowledge, enormous resources are spent to regulate schools and teachers through new penalties, increased oversight, and an overwhelming amount of curricular policy.

Curricular Policy

Curricular policy is the formal body of law and regulations that pertain to what should be taught in schools (Elmore & Sykes, 1992), including the values attached to this knowledge (Apple, 2004). Curricular policy research explores how official actions are determined,[5] what these actions require of schools and teachers, and how these actions affect what is taught to students. Curricular policy was created to intervene in the so-called failure of teacher education and to mask the new economics of the corporate state. However, the continued failure of teacher education to recognize its political entanglements leaves practicing teachers ill-equipped for the inevitable political work ahead (Oakes & Lipton, 2006). In this sense, teacher education has failed its democratic purpose.

Curricular policy research is a mélange of interests that examine curricula from many different perspectives. For instance, this body of work has examined governments' intentions for developing policy, coordination among agencies implementing curricular policy (state agencies, district offices, and schools), and teachers' interpretations and implementation of new curricular policy. Policy implementation became a particularly important type of scholarship because policy researchers needed a "more refined conception of the type of problems that follow from particular courses of action" (Elmore & Sykes, 1992, p. 192). In other words, what policy developers intend is not always what occurs in schools and classrooms.

Curricular policies eventually arrive on teachers' desks. What researchers observed was that teachers responded "in what often seemed quite idiosyncratic, frustratingly unpredictable, if not downright resistant ways" (McLaughlin, 1987, p. 172; see also Achinstein & Ogawa, 2006). Given these early findings, implementation studies noted that teachers

> are better understood as political brokers than as [curriculum] implementers. They enjoy considerable discretion, being influenced by their own notions of what schooling ought to be as well as persuaded by external pressures. This view represents a middle ground in the classic sociological contrast between professional autonomy and bureaucratic subordination. It pictures teachers as more of less rational decision-makers who take higher-level policies and other pressures into consideration in their calculation of benefits and costs. (Schwille et al., 1986, p. 377)

Implementation researchers noted that curricular policies entered schools with unique political environments, and these policies produced a set of "unpredictable outcomes of autonomous actors, motivated by self-interest" (McLaughlin, 1987, p. 177). What became clear in early implementation research was that (1) teachers exercised considerable power concerning policy outcomes and (2) their micropolitical resistance was conceptualized in the research as self-interested behavior rather than as a legitimate form of democratic resistance. Consequently, a significant area of micropolitical research examined the basis for teachers' resistance and power (see Reed, 2000).

Indeed, teachers have willingly complied with new curricular directives. That is to say, teachers have not, historically, resisted every single policy handed to them. However, even in cases of policy acceptance, teachers often graft on additional curricular and pedagogical techniques that stem from the poor practices that the policy intended to change in the first place (Ball, 1990). Realizing this, scholars have examined how teachers make sense of curricular policy and the ways they appropriately, or legitimately, resist poor policy (Patterson & Marshall, 2001). To compound matters, researchers noted that teachers are too frequently faced with implementing multiple policies at one time. Multiple policies that are poorly coordinated place pressure on teachers' limited time, reduce their opportunities to learn the curriculum, and increase their exposure to scrutiny and evaluation (Honig, 2006). In these circumstances, teachers resist policy to reduce the amount of work piled on in uncoordinated fashion and to reduce the intensification of surveillance brought about from that work.

Tightening up the coordination between schools and central agencies has been considered as one way to improve policy effectiveness and teacher compliance. However, calls to improve policy making (Whitty, 2006), policy implementation (Dumas & Anyon, 2006), and professional development opportunities (Borko, 2004) for teachers have replaced some emphasis on examining how central agencies and schools are "loosely coupled" (Weick, 1976) or how agencies coordinate curricular policy (Grossman & Thompson, 2004). This shift in research intent came about from the need to know about program outcomes rather than logistical coordination among agencies. Unfortunately, research that examines educators' micropolitics as a legitimate, and necessary, form of resistance is fairly recent (Johnson, 2004; Solomon, 2002). This form of research might be characterized as nascent expressions of a new democratic sensibility that micropolitically resists the hegemony of governments' desires. The spaces for democratic engagement are already in place.

The Birth of the (Micro)Political Pedagogue: Curricular Resistance

A new curriculum may threaten teachers if it challenges their beliefs about teaching and learning. Teachers construct many of their ideas about teaching and learning while they are students. Trying to change these beliefs has been a persistent problem in teacher education (Grossman, 1991). This problem, which is referred to as "the apprenticeship of observation," creates additional problems for both teachers and policy-makers (Lortie, 1975). One problem is that teachers' thoughts about teaching and learning that are based on their own experiences as students may perpetuate racist and sexist assumptions about how students learn. Another problem is that subject matter evolves (e.g., via technology), and teachers who rely on definitions of subject matter that were in use when they were students do a huge disservice to student learning. Finally, teachers have received less than adequate professional development opportunities to help them improve pedagogy or their understanding of subject matter. By definition, curricular policies contribute to a feeling of inadequacy among teachers (Borko, 2004).

Understanding why teachers resist or modify policy requires understanding the beliefs that guide their use of power. And, as I have argued, the power of teachers must be understood in relation to nomadism and the fractured landscapes they traverse. Simple characterizations of teachers' micropolitics as self-interested behavior neglect the territorializing environments of teachers' work, and the economic and military benefits that governments accrue by controlling this work. Teachers act politically in schools out of strong beliefs about the welfare of students. More importantly, teachers have exercised power to change how schools are organized so that they can maintain the pleasurable learning conditions they believe will benefit students.

Corbett's (1991) findings probably resonate with many people's experiences concerning how teachers respond to curricular policy:

> Regardless of what the formal curriculum says should be taught, closed classroom doors and the ubiquitous posters covering glass panels in the doors enable teachers to teach what and how they want. Thus teachers can dissent in practice to that which they are expected to assent in policy. (p. 76)

Corbett noted that teachers who perceived threats to their classroom autonomy ignored instructional changes when they believed these changes would reduce their classroom effectiveness. This is an important theme. Thirty-three years ago, Lortie (1975) argued that teachers were strongly motivated to protect their power, or autonomy, because it created opportunities for them to heighten their enjoyment of work. Lortie believed that classroom effectiveness was the largest incentive for teachers to continue working. He also speculated that teachers would seek to increase their power to maximize their *enjoyment* of solving instructional problems.

The pleasure teachers generate when solving instructional problems is integral to understanding their micropolitics (Zembylas, 2007). How many times have teachers described their commitment to teaching as "passionate"? Foucault (1983b) asked, "How can and must desire deploy its forces within the political domain and grow more intense in the process of overturning the established order?" (p. xii).

Micropolitical Pleasure

Moore-Johnson (1990) observed teachers who refused to comply to policy mandates because they enjoyed solving instructional problems. In this research, teachers enjoyed thinking through instructional problems with specific students, and this pleasure motivated them to continue teaching. Moore-Johnson reported that teachers desired control over what was taught, and how it was taught, because this allowed them to target specific students' needs. Moore-Johnson explained that teachers' resistance to curricular policy stemmed from tensions between what teachers believed to be generic policy platitudes that apply to all students and the specific teaching and learning needs of individual students (p. 136). In her study, teachers resisted, ignored, and threatened to quit as ways to reclaim their professional autonomy – or professional pleasure.

Reed's (2000) research on teacher power indicated further that teachers would engage in a number of political activities in schools to maintain preferred working conditions to assist students. Reed noted that the basis for teachers' micropolitical actions stemmed from four instructional concerns: students with learning problems, students with behavior problems, students who were physically and emotionally abused, and students with cultural (ethnic and class) differences. In many ways, the macropolicies were incomplete and did not account for the complex situations that teachers needed to account for in student learning (see also Patterson & Marshall, 2001). The enjoyment and pleasure of solving individual learning challenges was a significant factor in teachers' micropolitics.

Finally, Greenfield (1991) argued that teacher power was based "upon the beliefs of teachers ... regarding their perceived duty to serve the best interests of children" (p. 161). Greenfield's work indicated that teacher power is not simply relegated to classroom control – it affects school policy. In this case, teacher power can be thought of as an extremely influential force within schools. Greenfield claimed that teachers' power directed not only their political actions but also, when recognized by principals, the political authority of principals and the educational direction of the school.

Teachers' Micropolitics as Resistance to Surveillance

Teachers also resist curricular policies because of the attached assessment policies used to evaluate a policy's effectiveness (Bushnell, 2003). This becomes the clearest evidence of a soft form of teacher accountability. Oftentimes, these evaluations take the shape of high-stakes assessments of student learning. These measures direct the kind of instruction and school organization (grouping and tracking). Although there is some evidence that suggests that high-stakes tests can lead to improved student learning by directing instruction (Airasian, 1988), the overwhelming majority of this learning is aimed at helping students acquire basic skills, a trend that dangerously reduces teaching to a technical framework. Teachers are wary of the increased scrutiny that follows assessment systems that try to track student learning in such minimalist ways. It is not surprising that teachers refract surveillance in the form of high-stakes assessments when these assessments are attached to curricula that teachers resisted in the first place. This is exactly what Hargreaves (1991) found when he traced a new policy aimed to promote teacher collaboration in schools:[6]

> Administrative systems ... are less than fully serious about their rhetorical commitment to teacher [professionalization]. They are systems prepared to delegate to teachers and indeed hold them accountable for the collective, shared responsibility for [curriculum] implementation, while allocating to

themselves increasingly centralized responsibility for the development and imposition of educational purposes through curriculum and assessment mandates. They are systems of state regulation and control in which the business of conception and planning is increasingly separated from that of [teaching]. (p. 69)

Teachers' Micropolitics as Self-Interested Behavior

Unfortunately, some teachers exercise power poorly. That is, teachers use their power to insulate themselves from constructive changes to avoid answering hard questions concerning student well-being. They simply close the classroom door. There are no prima facie claims that teachers know better than curriculum developers and policy-makers about the needs of students. And the fragmentation and discontinuities of teacher education contribute to too many teachers not being adequately prepared to answer hard questions about student well-being (Darling-Hammond, 2006). At worst, teachers remain ignorant of these questions.

The schizophrenia that hovers over teachers' professional identity is exacerbated when teachers use their power to simply "survive" the political environment of schools instead of using their power to improve the conditions for themselves and their students (Blase & Anderson, 1995; Curry, Jaxon, Russell, Callahan, & Bicais, 2008; Keltchtermans & Ballet, 2002). Some teachers have spent more time protecting their self-interests by conforming to conventional values of the local community rather than improving the conditions for schooling (Blase, 1987b). Additionally, teachers build coalitions to ingratiate themselves with their peers rather than to achieve any apparent educational, curricular, or school purpose (Blase, 1987a). Noblit, Berry, and Demsey (1991) witnessed teachers exercising power to insulate themselves at two schools:

> The political power of teachers increased and negated the district's intent, but neither school was able to fashion a discussion of what teaching ought to be about. Each created its own folk concept of the profession. Dialogue about the professional beliefs is essential if teachers are to be effective societal voices about education and if they are to be a potent force in the macropolitics of schooling. (pp. 393-394)

To help, scholars have argued that teacher educators need to help teachers understand the organizational skills, knowledge, and commitments they must have if they are to reconcile school practices that conflict with their vision for students (Curry et al., 2008). New teachers are often taught pedagogical practices that clash with current school practices, particularly when new practices are intended to improve pedagogy. Thus, teachers need to be better prepared to resolve conflicts about teaching and learning in schools, particularly if teacher educators are imparting innovative pedagogies that schools (i.e., governments) do not support.

Summary

Teacher power is like a double-edged sword. On the one side, teachers exercise power to dismiss what they believe will not benefit them or their students. In this case, teacher power may be the single most effective deterrent to poor reform efforts since the end of the Second World War (Cuban, 1990). On the other side, teacher power can reinforce poor pedagogy through the wholesale rejection of innovative ideas. In this case, teacher micropolitics cuts in two ways: it affirms teachers' powerful status in regard to policy outcomes, but it raises questions about their reasons for resistance.

THE HARD ACCOUNTABILITY OF PERFORMANCE

Parallel to arguments about teachers' knowledge are disagreements about educators' roles in democratic societies. Educators' discretion could buffer, and perhaps ought to buffer, communities from government and corporate desires (Fenstermacher & Amarel, 1983). By inference, educational accountability ought to increase teachers' discretion and judgment to ensure freedom of thought in democracies. Interestingly, educators have been engaged in professional development activities to help them publicly demonstrate their work for years – a kind of public presentation of their nomadic journeys. For instance, video- and audiotapes (Little, 2003), networks (McDonald & Klein 2003), teacher action research (Cochran-Smith & Lytle, 1993), study groups (Supovitz, 2002), and mentoring (Athanases & Achinstein, 2003) are methods educators have used to visibly demonstrate their abilities.

However, calls for tighter educator accountability suggest that educators have done a poor job communicating the effects of these practices to policy-makers (Toll, 2002) and to themselves (Hiebert, Galimore, & Stigler, 2002). On the other hand, Wilcox and Finn (1999) dismissed professional development activities altogether because, they claimed, such territorializing attempts have no bearing on student performance. Finn and Wilcox (2000) argued that accountability systems that utilize student test scores provide the only kind of *visibility* that enables policy-makers to hold educators accountable. This form of visibility – data surveillance[7] – compels educators to comply with state and federal standards through the threat of sanction and the promise of rewards. States developed a "new accountability" (Fuhrman, 1999) and intended to make educators' work more visible through inspections, observations, performances, and public reporting of test scores – surveillance. Surveillance, then, becomes the tool of choice to more efficiently terraform teachers' knowledge landscapes and to economically track their nomadic journeys.

Territorialization Intent: Democratic Buffers or Bureaucratic Subordinates?

One axis of accountability research has tried to identify the purpose of educational accountability – who holds whom accountable for what. Early intent literature distinguished professional from bureaucratic[8] forms of accountability (Ingersoll, 2003), with the latter model closely related to models of market accountability (De Lissovoy & McLaren, 2003). Distinctions between these two broad forms of accountability rested on the clarification of roles and responsibilities for actors in the education drama. Because educational accountability was distributed across people and space (state agencies, district offices, classrooms, etc.), researchers argued that teachers held a role *sui generis* among other education professionals because of their (supposed) exclusive knowledge (see earlier discussion on teachers' displaced knowledges). This argument contended that educators' special knowledge of pedagogy, subject matter, and students distinguished their professional duties from others in the education bureaucracy. Thus, researchers concluded that any accountability system must relate appropriately to the work of educators, not administrators.

Researchers noted that educators' discretion simultaneously provided the material from which to evaluate educators and an important buffer to protect communities from state and corporate intrusion. Consequently, scholars argued that accountability frameworks should develop educators' discretion and, by inference, increase their professional autonomy to ensure freedom of thought in the democracy. However, critics speculated that accountability systems controlled by educators would be ineffective because educators would likely protect their power rather than use it to regulate themselves (McGivney & Haught, 1972). O'Day (2002) developed a hybrid form of education accountability in an attempt to marry performance and bureaucratic forms of accountability. Initial evidence of hybrid systems documents an escalation of accountability politics as governments and corporations prey on knowledge fissures for political and economic opportunities (Smith & Miller-Kahn, 2003). Finally, some critics have simply stated that performance accountability systems were designed to restore a neoconservative social agenda and a neoliberal economic agenda (Apple, 2006).

As noted earlier, governments have not been persuaded by arguments that teachers should control education policy. Initial evidence of hybrid systems documents an escalation of accountability politics as educators confront an erosion of power from state governments (Ingersoll, 2003) and the corporate community (Hargreaves, 2003). More importantly, the goal of performance accountability is not simply to suppress the teacher, even if this is what is occurring, "but rather to retool her" into a more effective instrument in economic production (Fraser, 1989, p. 24). The intent of accountability schemes is to coerce economic production by co-opting teachers into disciplinary power relations (Foucault, 1980b).[9]

Territorialization Effects: Capacity Building or Disciplining Technologies?

A second axis of accountability research examined the effects of accountability. The effects literature analyzed accountability systems in order to build better policy mechanisms – mechanisms to develop teachers' professional capacity (Darling-Hammond & Sykes, 1999) and/or mechanisms to punish and reward educators for their performances (Odden & Kelley, 2002). Recently, effects literature has switched its analytic focus away from educational bureaucracies to schools and educators. A "new accountability" developed to some extent because policy-makers honored earlier arguments about educators' unique roles (Fuhrman, 1999). That is, by focusing the accountability gaze onto schools and teachers (rather than the bureaucratic systems in which they where located), policy-makers were able to extract, or produce, schooling production more efficiently.

This so-called new performance accountability tried to make educators' work more visible through inspections, observations, performances, and the public reporting of test scores. Critics of performance accountability generally accepted the premise that *performance* was a legitimate construct of accountability[10] and instead challenged assumptions about the relationship between student achievement, educator performance, and test scores. For instance, some effects literature argued that test-driven accountability policies actually increased dropout rates for marginalized students (Whitford & Jones, 2000), perpetuated racist practices for language-minority students (Reyes & Rorrer, 2001), increased teacher demoralization (McNeil, 2000), and increased teachers' knowledge schizophrenia (Ball, 2003) – developments that constituted an abuse of professional subjectivity (Smyth, 2002; Zembylas, 2003) and the birth of multiple identities (Sachs, 2001), which compounded problems of teacher retention and nomadism (Ingersoll, 2003).

Effects literature also documented the widespread tracking practices of schooling related to economic production. Far too often student subjectivities have been predetermined, ranked, tracked, and in many cases commodified a priori. Performance learning is not about learning possibilities, it is about achieving what the accountability system has already determined are students' "realistic" identities and predetermined economic futures (DeLissovoy & McLaren, 2003). This has been particularly true for students who are systematically segregated through sorting practices such as (dis)ability (Baker, 2002), sexism (Kelly, 2003), and classism and racism (Kozol, 2005).

Critics of high-stake testing argued that such accountability systems only measured fiscal inequities between schools, not student achievement or educator effort. Even though school-funding formulas remain unequal and unconstitutional in several states in the United States (Wong, 1999), scholars noted that accountability decisions must be fair and equitable (Sirotnik, 2004). Thus, important legal questions have been raised concerning the responsibilities that states, governments, and districts have to support educators to fulfill accountability demands (Sirotnik & Kimball, 1999).[11] In the end, avowed conservatives believe that market economics (e.g., vouchers, choice programs) should settle the complexity of educational accountability (Wilcox & Finn, 1999).

Cultural Accountability: Who's in Control?

A third axis of accountability research is underway. This research examines educational accountability from the perspective of schools rather than the perspective of external mechanisms that expect to influence schools (Newmann, King, & Rigdon, 1997). The cultural literature assumed that schools have accountability systems already in place, albeit systems that may be unstated, ill-coordinated, and altogether different than what policy-makers and government bureaucrats desire. This literature examined how schools utilize local concepts of accountability and how educators make sense of accountability issues (Spillane et al., 2002).

Researchers noted how the cultural literature differed from both the effects literature and intent literature:

> Instead of asking how schools respond to policies designed to make them accountable to external authorities, we have asked how schools come to formulate their own conceptions of accountability and what role, if any, external policies play in these conceptions. Our working theory of accountability is predicated on the belief that external accountability systems operate on the margins of powerful factors inside the school, and that understanding these factors is a major precondition to understanding how and why schools respond the way they do to external pressures for accountability. (Abelmann & Elmore, 1999, p. 38)

The cultural literature is an important shift in the research on educational accountability. It provided evidence of accountability systems already in place in schools; it challenged arguments that maintained that educator accountability was absent or based on selfish interests; and it provided evidence of how the concept of accountability was a negotiated and choreographed set of practices between educators and policy-makers (Ball, 2003).

NOTES

1   Maurice Tabard, Man Ray, Claude Cahun, and Roger Parry created a series of photographs between 1928 and 1930 that explored the idea of multiple identities, or subjectivities. These photographs used solarization and double exposure to disrupt the idea that the individual has a core self. Instead, the subject possesses multiple identities produced through applications of power (San Francisco Museum of Modern Art, Stitch, 1990).

2   See for instance, http://news.bbc.co.uk/1/hi/in_depth/education/2000/bett2000/600667.stm and http://news.bbc.co.uk/1/hi/education/582475.stm

3   Alberto Giacometti developed a series of busts that explored the ways the skull was malleable. Here, the head can be easily shaped and formed – willing forms of cognitive plasticity.

4   Many of Max Ernst's landscapes were inspired as he witnessed the aftermath of the Second World War. In addition, his landscapes were also influenced by his experiences living in the southwest of the United States.

5   For instance, what issue the policy will address, who made that determination, and when it will be implemented. Frequently, but not always, curricular policies originate outside the school. Cochran-Smith and Susan Lytle (1993) argue that when policies originate outside the school this immediately places teachers in conflict with policy-makers about who has legitimate knowledge about students. These authors suggest that changes in curricula from teachers' perspectives would circumvent much of the problems associated with teacher resistance to outside policies.

6   In Hargreaves' example, teachers are again faced with making decisions about working more collaboratively with peers. Because assessments of teachers' behavior remain in the policy's hands, teachers resisted surveillance from both the policy and their peers. Hargreaves concluded that this policy really sought "contrived collegiality" and not a substantial form of teacher professionalism.

7 Data surveillance is "the collection of information about an identifiable individual [and organization], often from multiple sources, that can be assembled into a portrait of that person's activities" (Stanley & Steinhardt, 2003, p. 3).

8 Sometimes described as organizational accountability or administrative accountability.

9 As noted, a significant intention of performance accountability policies is to increase economic production and efficiencies for state and federal governments. Studies of "neoliberalism" and "neoconservatism" abound. However, the idea that education is subordinate to the economies of government is not new (Tyack, 1974). What is new is the way governments now hold teachers accountable to these economic desires. I have disproportionately represented this literature here for two reasons. First, the literature is very well articulated elsewhere, and articulated in great volume. Second, I have foreground micropolitics in this book as a way to compliment the macropolitical literature and as a way to fill the hole left by continued macroanalyses of educational policies. While I imagine some readers will find this deliberate omission distasteful, I hope other readers find it refreshing.

10 Some notable exceptions included Pignatelli (2002) and Gleeson and Husbands (2003).

11 See *Williams v. State of California* at http://www.ucla-idea.org.

CHAPTER 2

THE ANATOMY OF EDUCATION ACCOUNTABILITY

Theorizing Power as Assembling Subjectivity

In the previous chapter I discussed how, and why, governments hold schools accountable. I argued that teachers' fractured knowledge landscapes represent fertile territories for government colonization and that the territorializing wars over teachers' cognitions have produced golden opportunities for corporate states to ensure economic production in schools through teachers. However, I demonstrated that teachers sometimes resist macrodesires through micropolitical means.

The previous chapter discussed teachers' knowledge conflicts historically and asked the question, why have educators not been sufficiently prepared for these inevitable conflicts in their work? I argued that research should map these conflicts to inform educators (and teacher educators) about what others expect from their work; more importantly, I concluded that educators must be prepared to act as democratic buffers between macrodesires and the microspaces of democratic schooling. The continued absence of these discussions in teacher education remains an appalling feature of too many preparation programs.

This study, consequently, attempts to identify and analyze normative micropolitics among educators that resisted, or attempted to resist, government accountability structures. My assumption was that educators' micropolitical resistance was related directly, and produced directly, from the instantiation of power used to control them. In other words, I did not want to conflate *politics* with *power* in the research. I wanted to understand the form of power that lurked beneath performance accountability systems. How did this form of power operate? Would effective political resistance to this form of power operate as a contest at the macrolevel (Cole, 2003) or operate as an assortment of arts at the microlevel (Scott, 1990)? Would resistance occur at both levels (Vidovich, 2007), or does some intermediary space – a mezolevel – exist for resistance (Sibeon, 2004)?

Chapter Organization

In this chapter, I present my theoretical framework and its corresponding theory of action (theory of intention). The chapter proceeds in three parts. I first discuss how I conceptualized the idea of disciplinary power in relation to the measurement of school performance. I rely on the works of Michel Foucault (1977, 1980b) to explain how the disciplinary power of performance accountability operates as a technology of governmentality. Because I share some of Nancy Fraser's (1989) normative concerns about Foucault's ideas, I use her critique of these ideas to articulate the ways I operationalized ideas about teachers' intentions and subsequent actions.

In then discuss ideas of performativity that relate to surveillance and the production of organizational "truths" (Butler, 1990; Lyotard, 1984; Ball, 2003). In other words, I explore how the surveillance of schooling produces rituals for display purposes. More importantly, I discuss how performativity assembles educators' subjectivities through the self-fabrication "identity truths," for school surveillance produces "docile bodies" and assembles these compliant knowledge workers for more efficient education production. In this sense, educators' deterritorialized knowledges are "retooled" for the edu-economic production of the corporate state (Fraser, 1989, p. 27).

Finally, I build upon the discussion of performativity to examine ideas about educators' intentions and action. I briefly introduce the emerging politics of desire that is currently operating in schools through macrodecrees of educational performance (Peters, 2003). My goal is to understand how this visibility game can be appropriated and used in schools to disrupt and refract educational surveillance. This politics of subjectivity could produce a new ethic of schooling that has both libratory and catastrophic consequences.

Throughout this chapter, I use a number of schematics to ground theory into a breathing system of understanding.

POWER AND SOCIAL RELATIONS

Power is a widely used but nebulous construct in social science research. It has been defined as domination, resistance, authority, influence, force, and capacity. It has been considered something to acquire and something to avoid. Hobbes (1660/1982) argued for a singular sovereign power while French and Raven (1959) believed power emanated from everyone. Machiavelli (1513/1981) demonstrated how easy it was to influence sovereign power and warned that power would eventually consume those in authoritative positions. Bolman and Deal (1991) considered power the most important resource in organizations, and Pfeffer (1981) described power as the "property of the system at rest [while] politics is the study of power in action" (p. 7).

Arendt (1958) and Hartsock (1983) drew attention to the democratic and cooperative aspects of power that were (too) often left out of male theorists' conceptions.[1] Contemporary definitions stress the covert ways that power is used and how it is structured into social relations so that it does not appear to be used at all (Foucault, 1977; Lukes, 1974). Given its multiple meanings, theorists have questioned the utility of the concept (Dreyfus & Rabinow, 1982).

Perhaps the most frequently used definition of power originates from literature in political science. It states that power is evident when somebody is able to motivate somebody else to do something they would not have done otherwise. Dahl's (1961) study of key decision-making arenas focused on how power was used to resolve demonstrable conflicts: policy development in education, political nominations for local office, and an urban development proposal. Bachrach and Baratz (1970) critiqued Dahl's work, arguing that Dahl limited his attention to formal, observable decision-making arenas. Bachrach and Baratz believed that power is often used more covertly – behind closed doors. They believed that deals are struck "behind the scenes" to such a degree that some conflicts never reach a formal decision-making arena.

Lukes (1974) agreed that power was used both overtly and covertly, but he extended its definition. Lukes argued that these two early definitions of power focused too much on observable behavior or *potentially* observable behavior. Instead, he argued that power is much more difficult to observe because it can be used to shape people's interests in such a way that their interests remain latent and unexpressed. For Lukes, power shaped people's "perceptions, cognitions, and preferences in such a way that they accept their roles in the existing order of things" (p. 24).

The idea that power is structured into social practice (and in organizations, especially) is an attempt to understand how people are inculcated within a social practice or a set of social practices. The idea that power is structured in social practice is also an attempt to study how people are produced or inscribed with identity (e.g., "teachers," "students," "doctors," "criminals," and so on) (Foucault, 1977). Put differently, the idea that power is structured into social practice is an attempt to understand how people conform to dominant discourses (i.e., prevailing thought, language, and practices) and an attempt to understand the extent to which people can alter or resist the effects of disciplinary power. However, in order to resist the effects of power one must first understand how power colonizes cognition and fabricates desire.

Deterritorialized Knowledge Exploitation – Is it Pleasurable?

Lukes (1974) coined the phrase "the third face of power" and noted that people's interests and beliefs were shaped by dominant ideology. Lukes (1974) explained how ideology shaped preferences when he stated:

A may exercise power over B by getting him [*sic*] to do what he does not want to do, but he also exercises power over him by influencing, shaping or determining his very wants. Indeed, is it not the supreme exercise of power to get others to have the desires you want them to have – that is to secure their compliance by controlling their thoughts and desires? (p. 23)

The obvious connection here is that schools are places that need to organize, manage, control, and watch a growing number of students and educators. As demonstrated in the previous chapter, the regulation of students and educators has increasingly become a priority for the corporate state. More importantly, the new technologies of power seek to control the unconscious of people, or, put differently, technologies of power seek conformity by controlling people's thoughts and desires. Nietzsche (1968) noted this aspect of power when he stated, "Knowledge works as a tool of power … the measure of the desire for knowledge depends upon the measure to which the will to power grows in a species: a species grasps a certain amount of reality in order to become master of it, in order to press it into service" (Aphorism 480). Performance accountability is the current process used to effect the cognitive colonization of educators. And, of course, in relation to the economic concerns of the state, performance accountability is the contemporary technology used to corporatize students' cognitions as well (DeLissovoy & McLaren, 2003).

Foucault (1980b) argued that power was not always structured into social practices: the idea is a relatively new phenomenon of the last two centuries. Foucault argued that power was wielded initially by feudal lords, and, over time, these lords needed more efficient ways to control, order, and manage large numbers of people:

> In feudal societies power functioned essentially through signs and levies. Signs of loyalty to the feudal lords, rituals, ceremonies and so forth, and levies in the form of taxes, pillage, hunting, war, etc. In the seventeenth and eighteenth centuries a form of power comes into being that begins to exercise itself through social production and social service. It becomes a matter of obtaining productive service from individuals in their concrete lives. And in consequence, a real and effective "incorporation" of power was necessary, in the sense that power had to be able to gain access to the bodies of individuals, to their acts, attitudes and modes of everyday behavior ... These new techniques of power needed to grapple with the phenomena of population, in short to undertake the administration, control and direction of the accumulation of [people]. (p. 125)

The Organisation for Economic Co-operation and Development (OECD, 2007), in its *Education at a Glance,* noted the rapid increase in secondary-education attainment by people in its 22 member countries. The OECD is quick to point out how this rapid growth in "human capital stock" is ripe for economic utilization in member countries (p. 26). The report provides a comparison of the member countries' accountability systems that perpetuate the normative uses of surveillance to monitor schools (OECD, 2007, pp. 418-419). The OECD report confirmed Foucault's (1977) observation that state governments will produce docile bodies – that is, "human stock" – for economic utilization rather than for democratic emancipation.

Desirous Subjectivities and Willing Subjugation

A goal of panoptic power is to mask repression by positioning politics, or conflict, in such a way that people desire the repression that accompanies their bodily re-formation. In fact, Deleuze (1992) noted how people desire training re-formations as a result of ignorance about disciplinary power. He stated, "Many young people strangely boast of being 'motivated'; they re-request apprenticeships and permanent training. It's up to them to discover what they're being made to serve, just as their elders discovered, not without difficulty, the *telos* of the disciplines" (p. 7). Foucault (1982a) would often describe "willing" subjugation as a process of power reproduction, as the process of reproducing the intent of disciplinary power to subjugate people. Foucault, borrowing from Deleuze and Guattari (1983), commented, "the fascism in us all, in our heads and in our everyday behavior, [is] the fascism that causes us to love power, to desire the very thing that dominates and exploits us" (p. xiii).

Figure 6. René Magritte. The Lovers. 1928. © Estate of René Magritte / SODRAC (2008)

Deleuze (1992) reminded us that democratic, capitalist populations are malleable and training is the preferred method to continuously de-form and re-form its economic force:

Desire in never separable from complex assemblages that necessarily tie into molecular levels, form microformations already shaping postures, attitudes, perceptions, expectations, semiotic systems, etc. Desire is never an undifferentiated instinctual energy, but itself results from a highly developed, engineered setup rich interactions: a whole supple segmentarity that processes molecular energies and potentially gives desire a fascist determination ... It's too easy to be antifascist on the molar level, and not even see the fascist inside you, the fascist you yourself sustain and nourish and cherish with molecules both personal and collective. (Deleuze & Guattari, 1987, p. 215)

Democratic power can easily be subverted by masking fascist control through surveillance technologies and by coding its operation into schools. Max Ernst created his *The Angel of Hearth and Home* (below) as a direct representation and physical embodiment of fascism.[2] The seduction of capital through education and monitored through surveillance represents the co-optation of democratic interests and the social suicides that accompany such allure (Kozol, 2007; Loeb, 2007).

Figure 7. Max Ernst. The angel of hearth and home. 1937. © Estate of Max Ernst / SODRAC (2008)

Surveillance is one contemporary technology of disciplinary power that shapes people's desires. I discuss surveillance in terms of its analytic relations – capillary, efficient, and reproductive. The word "discipline" is used in the Foucauldian sense (1977), and I relate it to the ways that surveillance codes cognition and shapes desire: surveillance is discussed not only in terms of "privacy issues" but also in terms of *how* it colonizes epistemes.

DISCIPLINARY POWER

Clegg (1989) argued that the central feature of surveillance was its ability to obtain people's obedience by controlling their "private spaces" (p. 191). Drug testing,

Figure 8. Guillermo Meza. Eyes-paranoia. 1941. © Guillermo Meza / SODRAC (2008)

computer monitoring, surveillance cameras, and test data represent contemporary examples of this intent. Foucault (1977) understood surveillance to be part of a larger government technique to control and train growing populations. Foucault (1977) explained how surveillance operated, in relation to the larger ambition of disciplinary power, as the "means to correct training":

> The chief function of the disciplinary power is to "train," rather than to select … It does not link forces together in order to reduce them; it seeks to bind them together in such a way as to multiply and use them … It "trains" the moving, confused, useless multitudes of bodies and forces into a multiplicity of individual elements – small, separate cells, organic autonomies, genetic identities and continuities, combinatory segments. Discipline "makes" individuals; it is the specific technique of a power that regards individuals

both as objects and as instruments of its exercise ... it is a modest, suspicious power, which functions as a calculated, but permanent economy ... The success of disciplinary power derives no doubt from the use of simple instruments; hierarchical observation, normalizing judgement and their combination in a procedure that is specific to it, the examination. (p. 170).

Contrary to some scholars' ideas, the idea of surveiling educators and schools to hold them accountable is not a new idea (Fuhrman, 1999). Lortie (1975) discussed its nefarious micro-effects in schools 30 years ago. What is new is the scale of the education surveillance machine (e.g., state apparatuses of control) and the severity of threats tied to its coercive powers. The idea that schools are surveiled via high-stakes tests and levy a normalizing judgment (i.e., a performance score) is well documented in many countries in the English-speaking West (Earl, 1999; MacGillivray, Ardell, Curwen, & Palma, 2004; Shore & Wright, 2004).

In fact, what is new in macropolitical studies of the panoptic phenomenon is how the disciplinary machines of state governments and private groups are assembled together (Haggerty & Ericson, 2000). Accountability assemblages have been developed in the United Kingdom, the United States, Australia, and New Zealand (see Apple, Kenway, & Singh, 2005; Olssen, Codd, & O'Neill, 2004). So-called think tanks have paved the way for an unprecedented number of governmentality constellations in the United States that surveil schools through high-stakes tests. The Manhattan Institute, the Cato Institute, the American Enterprise Institute, the Heritage Foundation, the Business Round Table, and the Christian Coalition (to name just a few) all represent libertarian and conservative constellations that continuously surveil education (Apple, 2001). On a smaller scale, the Fraser Institute and the CD Howe Institute in Canada operate like their counterparts in the United States. And Ofsted and the National College of School Leadership in the United Kingdom are examples of direct government constellations that do the same. Societies of control exist throughout many representative democracies to hold education accountable to performance (Deleuze, 1992). What has not occurred, but seems inevitable, is the assemblage of a performance accountability war machine into a global network of education surveillance.

Deleuze and Guattari (1987) discuss the effects of assemblage in relation to power and desire:

There isn't a desire for power; it is power itself that is desire. Not a desire-lack, but desire as a plenitude, exercise, and functioning, even in the most subaltern of workers. Being an assemblage [agencement], desire is precisely one with the gears and the components of the machine, one with the power of the machine. And the desire that someone has for power is only his fascination with these gears, his desire to make certain of these gears go into operation, to be himself one of these gears – or, for want of anything better, to be the material treated by these gears, a material that is a gear in its own way. (p. 56)

What motivates this study is a desire to map the effects that surveillance has had on educators. My goal is to document how, or if, teachers have resisted the effects of surveillance. My goal is to try and develop a counter-politic to the surveillance of pedagogy. Of course, this needs to be done in relation to educators and schools. Foucault (1980b) helped me articulate my concerns when he suggested,

> Let us not ... ask why certain people want to dominate, what they seek, what is their overall strategy. Let us ask, instead, how things work at the level of on-going subjugation, at the level of those continuous and uninterrupted processes which subject our bodies, govern our gestures, dictate our behaviours, etc. In other words, rather than ask ourselves how the sovereign appears to us in his lofty isolation, we should try to discover how it is that subjects are gradually, progressively, really and materially constituted through a multiplicity of organisms, forces, energies, materials, desires, thought, etc. (p. 97)

Becoming Productive: Assembling Docile Subjects through Terror

Historically, teachers have been considered guileful, deceitful, and desirous, which has prompted surveillance systems designed to hold them accountable to external policy (Warren, 1968). Warren (1968) believed that teachers should be surveiled because they often complied with organizational procedures without significant action or investment on their part. Essentially, argued Warren, teachers easily said one thing but did another. Warren hypothesized that surveillance was a more effective way to hold teachers accountable than devoting time to acquire symbolic acceptance of school policy. Surveillance provided administrators with ways to coerce teachers through "the expectation of punishment for failure to conform to an influence attempt" (p. 953).

Foucault (1980b) examined the relationship between surveillance and the inculcation of people's preferences. In his words, he examined "the point where power reaches into the very grain of individuals, touches their bodies and inserts itself into their actions and attitudes, their discourses, learning processes and everyday lives" (p. 39). Foucault argued that surveillance "circulated" within a social body and coercion was a property of organizational relationships exercised through the threat of being seen. The significance of this idea was that people were implicated in their own disciplining; they desired their own cognitive colonization. Foucault described how people tended to regulate themselves in proportion to the promise of being seen:

> All that is needed then is to place a supervisor in a central tower and to shut up in each cell a madman, a patient, a condemned man, a worker, or a school boy ...Hence the major effect of the Panopticon [is] to induce in the inmate a state of conscious and permanent visibility that assures the automatic functioning of power. So to arrange things that the surveillance is permanent inmates should be caught up in a power situation of which they are themselves the bearers. (pp. 200-201)

The installation of cameras on local metro busses to reduce crime is another example of a panoptic technology. The camera does not even have to work properly to have the intended effect of people self-regulating their behavior (that is, the camera may not be "plugged in"). One-way mirrors are also panoptic technologies.

More to the point of the present research, consider the potential effect of unannounced principal supervisory visits on classroom teachers or the use of high-stakes achievement tests in state-wide accountability systems. Parental help in the classroom also has unintended effects on teacher performance when parents act as panoptic surveillance for other parents, principals, and districts. Finally, students can operate as surveillance technologies when they provide (mis)information to guardians about schools and educators (Corbett, 1991). However, the covert micropolitical uses of surveillance should not be read as the only form of school surveillance. Schools have been quite explicit about their use of surveillance to control students. However, this book is about surveillance used on, and by, teachers.

THE ANATOMY OF SCHOOL SURVEILLANCE: MICROSPACES OF TERROR AND COERCION

The surveillance of educators' knowledge – the concerted effort to expose and exploit teachers' thinking – occurs through two spaces of coercion. Lyotard (1984) considered "terror" the primary mechanism of educational coercion when he said:

> By terror I mean the efficiency gained by eliminating, or threatening to eliminate, a player from the language game one shares with him. He [*sic*] is silenced or consents, not because he has been refuted, but because his ability to participate has been threatened. The decision makers' arrogance consists in the exercise of terror. It says: "Adapt your aspirations to our ends – or else." (p. 63)

The first dimension of coercion, terror, is produced through explicit macropolitical monitoring of performance data, which is understood in many professional fields as data surveillance and data mining. Governmental monitoring of performance data is accompanied by threats of school closure, school reconstitution, teacher dismissal, and penalties of reduced school income – all of which threaten schools and teachers with financial vulnerability or loss of careers. Of course, the use of terror need not always be used explicitly through macropolitical performance indicators. Surveiling unspoken expectations produces the second dimension of coercion. Unannounced visits by principals, for instance, regulate teachers through local, often unspoken, school or community norms and generic codes of the profession. Consequently, micropolitical uses of surveillance-terror produce a flow of pedagogical performances through acquiescence; teachers have historically, and consistently, conformed to pervasive ideology from fear of ostracism more than fear of overt punishment (Lortie, 1975).

Foucault (1980b) developed a framework, or what he called a "grid of analysis which makes possible an analytic relations of power," to depict how surveillance operated (p. 199). For Foucault (1977), the framework expressed itself

> as a tactics of power that fulfills three criteria: first, to obtain the exercise of power at the lowest possible cost [efficient]; second, to bring the effects of ... power to their maximum intensity and to extend them as far as possible [capillary]; third ... to increase the docility and the utility of all the elements of the system [reproductive]. (p. 218)

I have illustrated the three elements of Foucault's thought in Figure 9. The figure represents the x-, y-, and z-axes of Foucault's grid. In theory, the placement of a given act in the three-dimensional space depends on the extent of the efficient, reproductive, or capillary action it represents.

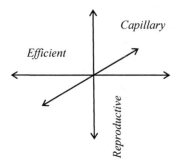

Figure 9. Constituent elements of surveillance.

Summary

There is a certain dialectical element involved in technologies of disciplinary power (e.g., cameras, towers, and accountability policies). By virtue of the technology, people respond to it; by virtue of how people act, technologies are adjusted. Those being watched are their own watchers. People control themselves even in cases where the technology does not work properly. Likewise, those watching are regulated by the technology and subject to administrative control. This "to and fro" or "give and take" quality of disciplinary power illustrates that power is continuous, anonymous, and productive.

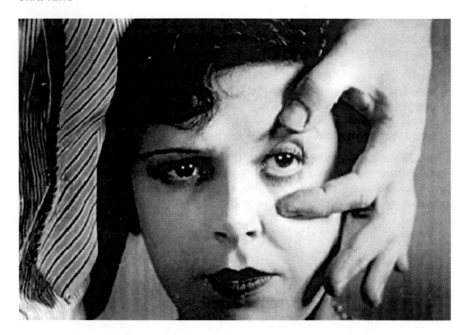

Figure 10. Luis Buñuel and Salvador Dalí. Un chien Andalou. 1929. (Still image). ©
Salvador Dalí, Fundació Gala-Salvador Dalí / SODRAC (2008)

So far, I have described surveillance as the means to produce more standardized and efficient teachers. And, of course, the goal of disciplinary power is to induce a desire for such re-formation.[3] Even though surveillance explains how interests are held accountable to pervading discourses (e.g., performance standards), surveillance, by itself, does not explain the process of fabricating desires. To better understand how surveillance fabricates desires, it is helpful to understand the performance pressure associated with its effects. This idea is directly tied to province- and state-wide performance accountability systems. By understanding the pressures of performance, or what some authors call "performativity," fabricated interests can be explained and better understood in micropolitical analyses (Ball, 2001, 2003).

ASSEMBLING COGNITIONS, PERFORMING TEACHERS

Everything is political, but every politics is simultaneously a *macropolitics* and a *micropolitics*.

– Gilles Deleuze and Félix Guattari,
A Thousand Plateaus

Ball (2001) described the current performance-accountability game as a "tactics of transparency [that] produce a resistance of opacity" (p. 211). This game relies on two important rules that govern who observes the performance and the way in which the performance is interpreted. Ball (2001) described the complexity associated with these two rules:

> There is not so much, or not only, a structure of surveillance, as a flow of performativities both continuous and eventful. It is not the certainty of being seen that is the issue. Instead it is the uncertainty and instability of being judged in different ways, by different means, through different agents; the "bringing-off" of performances – the flow of changing demands, expectations and indicators that make us continually accountable and constantly recorded. (pp. 211-212)

Goals, objectives, and standards are prevalent and pervade discourses that shape the ritualized performance of the appraisal meeting, annual review, observation, and inspection.

Ball (2003) noted that "the management of performance ... is 'called up' by inspection. What is produced is a spectacle, or game-playing, or cynical compliance, or what one might see as an 'enacted fantasy,' which is there simply to be seen and judged – a fabrication" (p. 222). Butler (1990) commented that "acts, gestures, enactments, generally construed, are performative in the sense that the essence or identity that they otherwise purport to express are fabrications manufactured and sustained through corporeal signs and other discursive means" (p. 66). Fabrications (e.g., test scores), then, are micropolitical performances circulated within schools to refract macropolitical gazes. Over time, Ball (2001) observed how performativity co-opts the organization's interests when coalitions transform their practice into the accumulation of signs, or fabrications:

> Organizational fabrications are an escape from the gaze, a strategy of impression management that in effect erects a façade of calculation. It is, as few have seen, a betrayal even, a giving up of claims to authenticity and commitment, it is an investment in plasticity. Crucially and invariably acts of fabrication and the fabrications themselves act and reflect back upon the practices they stand for. The fabrication becomes something to be sustained, lived up to. Something to measure individual practices against. (p. 217)

Fabrication as Micropolitical Strategy

Within organizations, many of us have participated in the gathering or creation of "evidence" to satisfy performance expectations, and we often use the corporate value of "efficiency" to guide our production as we create the minimum amount of artifacts intended to satisfy all of the criteria. Educators acquire preferences for fabrications because of the correct local, cultural, or organizational meaning they denote in schools (Kelchtermans & Ballet, 2002). In other words, the status quo is maintained by virtue of mitigating, indeed eliminating, alternatives to the status quo through the surveillance of the performance of predetermined standards.

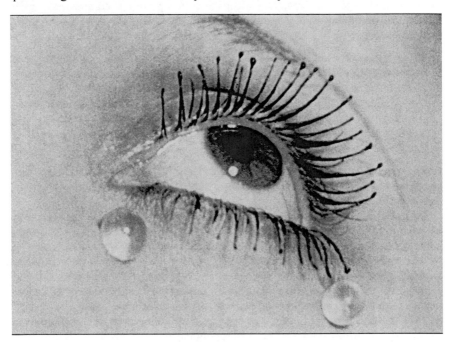

Figure 11. Man Ray. Tears. 1930-1932. (Optical performance/fabrication.) © Man Ray Trust / SODRAC (2008)

Pedagogical fabrications are created to be seen and judged; they are Baudrillardian (1981) signs circulated within the surveillance systems of schools. Educators create fabrications to control surveillers' impressions of their work; they engage in adept micropolitical tactics to (re)control their knowledge and (re)control the meaning of their professional status – or what Deleuze and Guattari (1987) would describe as a "micropolitics of perception, affection, conversation, and so forth" (p. 213). Thus, teachers' fabrications are strategies to reterritorialize their knowledge – they constitute a "new" set of cognitive microstrategies to refract the accountability gaze and a ubiquitous tactic to close the classroom door.

Fabrications are evidence of educator resistance produced from the panoptic gaze to refract the surveillance effects of performance accountability. Pedagogical fabrications momentarily shape surveillers' impressions – throw a wrench in the panoptic machine – and "define innumerable points of confrontation, focuses of instability, each of which has its own risks of conflict, of struggle, and of an at least temporary inversion of the power relation" (Foucault, 1977, p. 27). Educator fabrications are micropolitical responses intended to insurrect teachers' increasingly subjugated knowledge. Indeed, pedagogical fabrications can be seductive performances circulated within schools in order to obfuscate accountability gazes.

Figure 12. Man Ray. Noire et blanche. 1926. © Man Ray Trust / SODRAC (2008)

The uncertainty of being judged in different ways by different surveilers frames how educators present their work. As a result, fabrications are micropolitical approximations intended to present oneself within contested performance geographies that comply, or literally are "seen to comply," with accountability expectations. A politics of representation, therefore, becomes an integral way to understand how the audit culture produces subjectivity (Mehan, 2001). In his work, Man Ray captured the idea of subjectivity and the desire to (consciously) select multiple and different – and, depending on the times – "exotic" or "erotic" identities.

As forms of impression management, educators' performances are political because they attempt to (re)control, or (re)claim, the discourse of what a "good" teacher does and/or is. Jones and Pittman (1982) identified five prevalent impression management techniques that individuals often use to create "reality":

• ingratiation: individuals use flattery to be seen as likeable
• self-promotion: individuals play up their abilities to appear competent

- exemplification: individuals meet and exceed expectations to appear dedicated
- supplication: individuals advertise their shortcomings to be viewed as needy
- intimidation: individuals seek to appear threatening to be viewed as dangerous

Impression management is a way (that is, one way) to strategically respond to (or refract) the surveillance of pedagogy. Readers might imagine this as deciding which mask to wear, and deciding in which situation to wear it. Deleuze and Guattari (1987) discussed micropolitics in just this way when they noted, "there is a micropolitics of perception, affection, conversation, and so forth" (p. 213). Viewed in this way, ideas about impression management relate well with ideas of cognitive politics (Anderson, 1991), strategic interaction (Goffman, 1969), the politics of representation (Mehan, 2001), and the politics of subjectivity (Ransom, 1997).

Schizoanalytics and Bodies Without Organs

> The body is the body. Alone it stands. And in no need of organs. Organism it never is. Organisms are the enemies of the body.

> – Antonin Artaud, quoted in Deleuze and Guattari (1987)

The risks associated with impression management carry a heavy burden. For instance, Woods and Jeffrey (2002) discovered that teachers suffered from strained psychics when they engaged in cognitive politics inside schools. Woods and Jeffrey (2002) described teachers as possessing "multiple selves" and "restructured identities" when they fabricated organizational expectations. Ball (2003) also noted cognitive crises of performativity that act as a kind of "values schizophrenia" for educators. In this sense, interests are shaped from, and fabricated into, the disciplinary discourse of performance. Foucault (1977) explained the logical outcome of restructuring:

> The individual is no doubt the fictitious atom of an "ideological" representation of society; but he [*sic*] is also a reality fabricated by this specific technology of power that I have called "discipline." We must cease once and for all to describe the effects of power in negative terms: it "excludes," it "represses," it "censors," it "abstracts," it "masks," it "conceals." In fact, power produces; it produces reality [interests, shared or otherwise]; it produces domains of objects [organizational coalitions] and rituals of truth [rational negotiations]. (Foucault, 1977, p. 194)

As Fraser (1989) noted, the goal of accountability is not simply to subjugate the educator "but rather to retool her" into a more effective instrument in education production. In this sense, educators are "the vehicles of power, not its points of application" (Foucault, 1980b, p. 98). Assembled together, teaching bodies (bodies as objects) represent the new disciplinary force of corporate state control. Deleuze and Guattari (1987) explained how the surveillance machine assembles bodies (without organs) through fabrications:

> There are a number of questions. Not only how to make oneself a BwO [body without organs], and how to produce the corresponding intensities without which it would remain empty (not exactly the same question). But also how to reach the plane of consistency. How to sew up, cool down, and tie together all the BwO's [sic]. If this is possible to do, it is only by conjugating the intensities produced on each BwO, by producing a continuum of all intensive continuities. Are not assemblages necessary to fabricate each BwO, is not a great abstract Machine necessary to construct the plane of consistency? (p. 158)

The artist Hans Bellmer often represented restructured, or re-formed, body assemblages in his work. Bellmer's sculptures articulate the material effects of bodily reconstruction. In this sense, Bellmer's sculptures physically represent the more general idea of the body as object and, for my purposes, the more specific teacher as object – Foucault's docile body, Fraser's retooled body, and Deleuze and Guattari's BwO. Given the predominance of female teachers in the world, Bellmer's *Doll* (below) is an accurate portrayal of the violent effects done to teachers through performance accountability structures.

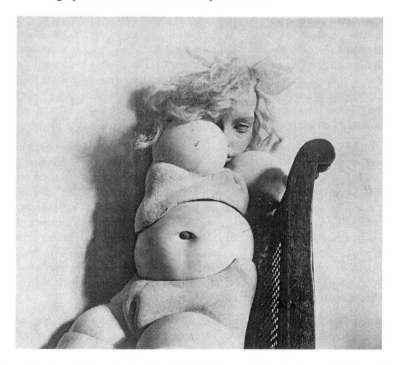

Figure 13. Hans Bellmer. Doll. 1934-1935. © Estate of Hans Bellmer / SODRAC (2008)

Schizoanalytics

Deleuze and Guattari (1987) noted that the schizophrenia that developed from capitalist fabrications could be analyzed through *schizoanalysis*. Schizoanalysis comprises four components that attempt to identify the different signs used in micropolitical representations. Delueze and Guattari (1987, p. 146) outlined the components of schizoanalysis as follows: (1) the generative, which is the study of concrete mixed semiotics; (2) the transformational, which is the study of pure semiotics; (3) the diagrammatic, which is the study of abstract machines; and (4) the machinic, which is the study of assemblages that effectuate abstract machines.

The ideas of schizoanalysis are rooted in descriptions of actions – descriptions of micropolitical semiotics – that interact with forms of disciplinary power designed to regulate people through visibility threats. However, micropolitical semiotics are often described as solitary endeavors, which says much about the (re)formational aspects of creating docile bodies (BwOs, (re)structured selves, assembled cognitions) for a more productive self capable of fulfilling the capitalist project more efficiently. Could micropolitical semiotics be used to resist a capitalist hegemony collectively? How? Smith (2005) pondered:

> If, as Deleuze and Guattari suggest, schizophrenia appears as the illness of our era, it is not as a function of generalities concerning our mode of life, but in relation to very precise [disciplinary] mechanisms of an economic, social and political nature ... The schizophrenic is like the limit of our society, but a limit that is always avoided, reprimanded, abhorred. The problem of schizophrenia [and schizoanalysis] then becomes: how does one prevent the breakthrough from becoming a breakdown? ... Is it possible to utilize the power of a lived chemistry and a schizo-logical analysis to ensure that the schizophrenic process does not turn into its opposite, that is, the production of the schizophrenic found in the asylum? If so, within what type of group, what kind of collectivity? (p. 190)

Might the fabrication process be subverted? If so, how? Writers have been quick to point out that Foucault did not sufficiently discuss the role of agency and intentionality in relation to power (Dreyfus & Rabinow, 1982). Foucault was interested in how power "transforms human beings into subjects" and not how people resist, transmit, or otherwise use power (Foucault, 1982a). This particular focus leaves unanswered questions about how, or if, people exercise power when power is structured in social practices. Nancy Fraser (1989) argued that Foucault's project, while extremely helpful, was not "capable of specifying who is dominating or subjugating whom and who is resisting or submitting to whom" (p. 29). I partially agree with Fraser. However, Foucault (1982a) did not avoid the issue. He recognized the need to talk about these concerns:

> The relationship between power and freedom's refusal to submit cannot therefore be separated. The crucial problem of power is not that of voluntary servitude. At the very heart of the power relationship, and constantly provoking it, are the recalcitrance of the will and the intransigence of

freedom. Rather than speaking of an essential freedom, it would be better to speak of an "agonism" – of a relationship which is at the same time reciprocal incitation and struggle; less of a face-to-face confrontation which paralyzes both sides than a permanent provocation. (pp. 221-222).

Foucault understood people's relationships with power to be a constant struggle, a struggle that is made permanent by our continued calls for freedom. To understand this tension, Foucault (1982a) believed that researchers should analyze micropolitics by "focusing on carefully defined institutions," because institutions exercise power relations to the highest efficacy (p. 222).[4]

RESEARCHING MICROPOLITICAL SEMIOTICS IN SCHOOLS

Make a map, not a tracing. The orchid does not reproduce the tracing of the wasp; it forms a map with the wasp, in a rhizome ... The map does not reproduce an unconscious closed in upon itself; it constructs the unconscious.

– Deleuze and Guattari, *A Thousand Plateaus*

There is nothing mystical about fabricating educators' interests. This point is emphasized when individuals and coalitions use a variety of strategies to socially construct "reality." From cognitive politics to impression management to micropolitical semiotics, the school is a site that is recreated over and over in relation to the macropolitical (Blase, 1991). What is really at stake when researching stealth forms of power in schools is the extent to which educators are aware of the structures that fabricate their intentions and subsequently shape their agency.

Macro- and Micropolitics: Issues of Educational Sovereignty and Accountability

There is little consensus about what defines phenomena as uniquely micropolitical and distinct from those which are "macropolitical" . . . Much that is now defined as specifically "micropolitical" is hardly distinguishable as uniquely "political" human interaction.

– Hanne B. Mawhinney, "Reappraisal"

In short, everything is political, but every politics is simultaneously a *macropolitics* and a *micropolitics*. (italics original)

– Deleuze and Guattari, *A Thousand Plateaus*

The juxtaposition of the above quotations reveals divergent ideas about the binaries of macro- and micro-. The primary difference between the two quotations rests on the extent to which identifying features (e.g., juridical, legislative, economic, cognitive, etc.) distinguish macro- and micro-environments from each other and the extent to which political action can be understood within such distinctions. No easy task. Mawhinney (1999) suggested that there could be, and probably ought to be, distinct features that qualify something as uniquely macro- and, hence, micro-.

Mawhinney (1999) suggested that micropolitical action could be derived deductively from mapping supposedly individual macro- and microterrains. On the other hand, Deleuze and Guattari (1987) suggested that the territorial borders are symbiotic and produce a politic in collapsed, or symbiotic, binaries (macro- *and* micro-). These conceptual differences regarding the territories of teachers' work are generated from thinking about power as something that operates in stealth; thus, they produce divergent research trajectories for the study of educational micropolitics. These incompatible trajectories raise different questions and produce different forms of data. The two divergent methodological approaches can summarized as (1) ways to partition macro- and microjurisdictions and develop concomitant notions of politics related to jurisdiction and (2) ways to understand political action produced from a symbiosis of macro- and microjurisdictions. The bold line in Figure 14 locates the school within a contested landscape, while the dotted lines represent the methodological debate between demarcated or permeable territories. I examine both methodological trajectories and identify how concomitant ideas of *agency* are developed to support respective conceptions of macro- and micro-.

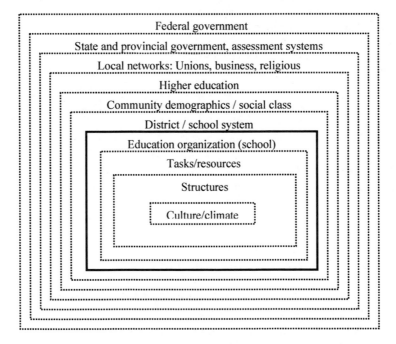

Figure 14. A representation of macro- and micro-environments in education.

Political Territories in Education and the Cultural Isomorphs of Schools

Sovereign, law and prohibition formed a system of representation of power which was extended during the subsequent era by the theories of right: political theory has never ceased to be obsessed with the person of the sovereign. Such theories still continue today to busy themselves with the problem of sovereignty. What we need, however, is a political philosophy that isn't erected around the problem of sovereignty, nor therefore around the problems of law and prohibition. We need to cut off the King's head: in political theory that has still to be done.

– Foucault, *Power/knowledge*

Figure 14 represents one way to territorialize educational macro- and micro-environments.[5] Typically, distinctions between these two environments are articulated by identifying roles, responsibilities, and interests within purportedly separate educational arenas (represented as nests). The significance of territorializing macro- and microterritories rests with understanding who is accountable to whom, and for what. As Foucault (1980b) noted, the methodological preoccupation of territorializing the macro- rests with determining who has sovereign legitimacy and who does not. In any event, once macro- and microterritories are demarcated in some fashion – for instance, as in Figure 14 – empirical data can then be gathered in an attempt to map how power operates between contested territories.

To support conceptions of separate territories, notions of agency attach identifiable interests to actors to explain political behavior. Power is used to explain the eventual clash of competing or conflicting interests. We could think of this as an "interest-based" or "identity-based" politics. Identity-based politics is an idea that is frequently used in micropolitical research, and it is operationalized as interest groups due to the popular idea that groups have "more" power than individuals (Bacharach & Mundell, 1993). Constituencies are formed from either shared interests or mutual interests in cases where the coalition is used as a temporary vehicle to achieve independent goals (Malen, 2001). Thus, organizational politics can be traced as a set of actions (i.e., strategies) used by coalitions to acquire, or otherwise use, said interests within the organization (Johnson, 2001).

The configuration of separate territories, consequently, produces micropolitical analyses that are intersectional in nature. The intersectional nature is is evident when opposing coalitions try to and resolve conflicts – or, put another way, try to resolve conflict with an essentialized other. Political action, then, is predicated on isomorphic[6] identities correlated with, or fixed to, a specific location on a territorialized map:

- [teachers] vis-à-vis [policy-makers]
- [teachers] vis-à-vis [parents]

Compound isomorphic identities could also be formed by combining territorial jurisdictions:

- [{female} {principal}] vis-à-vis [{male} {teachers}]
- [{black} {activist}] vis-à-vis [{white} {superintendent}]
- [{poor} {families}] vis-à-vis [{wealthy} {communities}]

The intersectional aspects of micropolitics are reproduced, and reinforced, once interests are ascribed to particular groups. Identity politics, consequently, is limited only to the extent that competing or conflicting interests can be ascribed to particular groups.

REMAPPING POWER IN EDUCATIONAL MICROPOLITICS

Power must be analyzed as something which circulates.

– Foucault, *Power/knowledge*

Deleuze and Guattari (1987) provided a different conception of micropolitics than the one that results from interest groups that emanate from distinct territories. The authors' conception of collapsed territories redirected attention toward the symbiotic relationship between macro- and micro-environments. As a result, the authors' conception of power and political action is different. With this shift, Deleuze and Guattari (1987) focused attention on how conceptions of micropolitics are produced and maintained in traditional micropolitical analyses. More importantly, Deleuze and Guattari (1987) utilized a very different theory of power to support their conception. To understand that political action developed from a symbiotic relationship between macro- and micro- is to understand how micropolitical interests can be fabricated in the macropolitical. Hence, political action results from, and is enacted within, the macro- *and* micro-.

The attempt to dissolve territorial boundaries is not an attempt to deny the existence of structures and territories that demarcate macro- and micro-arenas in education. Hardly. One would be hard pressed to deny state and provincial regulation of schooling, for instance. Or, for example, it would be difficult to deny the unequal funding of education and its grotesque impact on public schooling (Kozol, 2005). Schools are located within strong structures and prevalent territories. The dissolution of territorial boundaries is instead an attempt to reveal how power circulates throughout macro- and micro-environments simultaneously, rather than simply within territorialized jurisdictions. Giddens (1984), for instance, provided one collapse point when he argued that interests are not independent of the structures they inhabit – they are often shaped by these very structures.

It should be no surprise, then, that interests and interest groups can be fabricated through the management of organizational structures. This was Lukes' (1974) point when he made the following speculation:

A may exercise power over B by getting him [*sic*] to do what he does not want to do, but he also exercises power over him by influencing, shaping or determining his very wants. Indeed, is it not the supreme exercise of power to get others to have the desires you want them to have – that is to secure their compliance by controlling their thoughts and desires? (p. 23)

Instead of understanding power as located and operationalized within specific territories and with "core" or essentialized interests, panoptic forms of power create opportunities to understand how power fabricates interests to produce micropolitical action. However, we could say that the research area of micropolitics is still wedded to the epistemological roots of determining the sovereignty of democratic power, as four centuries of debate about Hobbes and Machiavelli suggest.

Cut off the King's Head: Stealth Forms of Power and the Fabrication of Interests

[Individuals] are not only its inert or consenting target; they are always also the elements of its articulation. Individuals are the vehicles of power, not its points of application.

– Foucault, 1980b, *Power/knowledge*

What types of units of analysis have been produced from conceptions of power as covert and panoptic? In what ways has *agency* been co-opted from stealth forms of power? Figure 15 distinguishes between stealth forms of power that operate in schools. One side of the continuum represents covert forms of power that are not witnessed (and are often not known).

| *Covert* | *Panoptic, invisible* |
| [Potentially witnessed] | [Not observable, manifest in desires] |

Figure 15. Continuum of stealth forms of power and micropolitical visibility.

Covert forms of power also represent political action that attempts to maintain decision making in opaque forums. However, covert forms of power could be observed. The right side of the continuum represents invisible forms of power that shape peoples' desires. Panoptic forms of power cannot be seen but are manifest in the unconscious of people through behavior. The introduction of a radical interiority of power disrupts notions of isomorphic interests and self-directed agency developed from intrinsic, core, essential, or otherwise self-aware and self-protected politics. Accounting for forms of power that are covert and radically interior suggests that micropolitical interests are manipulated and fabricated because interests can be obscured from individuals and groups and, more importantly, because interests can be produced. Thus, panoptic forms of power fabricate interests through macropolitical mechanisms to achieve micropolitical ends.

Figure 16 represents possible units of analysis that are neglected in micropolitical analyses as a result of territorializing legislative and cognitive spaces. One end of the spectrum represents covert instances of power, and the corresponding units of analysis are the ways organizational structures are reproduced. For example, school governance models (i.e., site councils) have been identified as extensions of state and provincial control rather than, as they are advertised, powerful local constituencies (Malen & Ogawa, 1988). On the other end of the spectrum, once power is conceived as operating panoptically, the units of analysis become the ways in which interests are fabricated and performed within the organization. These types of units of analysis map the production of desire.

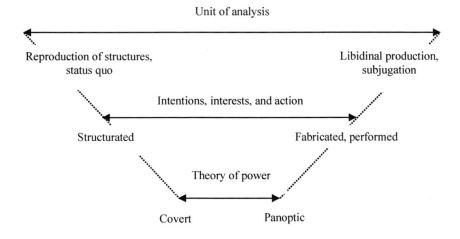

Figure 16. Mapping units of analysis onto stealth conceptions of power.

THE STRUCTURATION OF EDUCATORS' MICROPOLITICAL ACTIONS

People know what they do; they frequently know why they do; but what they don't know is what they do does.

– Foucault, "The Subject and Power"

Four axioms guided my thinking about teachers' micropolitical semiotics.

Axiom 1. Educators socially construct their working realities in relation to both the macro- and microstructures in which their work is located (e.g., calendars, budgets, architecture, gender, race, accountability policies, and so on).

Lukes (1977) noted the methodological implications of this idea when he stated:

> Social life can only properly be understood as a dialectic of power and structure, a web of possibilities for agents, whose nature is both active and structured, to make choices and pursue strategies within given limits ... Any standpoint or methodology which reduces that dialectic to a one-sided consideration of agents without ... structural limits or structures without agents, or which does not address the problem of their interrelation, will be unsatisfactory. (p. 29)

The first methodological implication is related to how educators' interests are shaped according to the macro-environment and the various micro-codes of the organization (Giddens, 1984). Thus, conceptions of agency are enacted within the structures that produce it, or "where structure is conceived as both the medium and the outcome of social practice" (Foster, 1989, p. 23). The first axiom seeks more nuanced accounts of how educators' interests are shaped by the macro-environment and the micro-codes of the organization; it seeks richer descriptions of how micropolitical action is produced and performed within these symbiotic structures.

Axiom 2. Because notions of agency are structured, stealth forms of power represent the segmentation of power.[7]

This axiom replaces a popular conception that power is "distributed" in schools (i.e., the concept of distributive leadership). Power segmentation represents power as a property rather than as a resource of the organization. The distinction between segmentation and distribution seeks clearer descriptions of how power is coded into organizations (i.e., historically, normatively, through policy, and so on). More emphatically, the distinction reveals how organizational coding subjugates desires and, subsequently, produces action, resistance, or compliance. The second axiom, then, seeks more detailed accounts of how the macro-environment shapes organizational members' interests and the ways these interests are performed within the organization.

The idea that power is segmented in schools raises methodological issues about agency in schools. The extent to which people are aware of the segmentation of power is the third axiom.

Axiom 3. The segmentation of power reproduces a striation of cognition.

While structuration theory provides a way to understand agency within segmented structures, the degree to which agents are conscious of such structures is not apparent. Perhaps we could theorize strong and weak forms of structuration, wherein strong forms document the unconscious subjugation of educators as their interests become fabricated. This was one of Foucault's (1980b) projects. He noted:

> Let us not ... ask why certain people want to dominate, what they seek, what is their overall strategy. Let us ask, instead, how things work at the level of on-going subjugation, at the level of those continuous and uninterrupted processes which subject our bodies, govern our gestures, dictate our behaviours etc. In other words, rather than ask ourselves how the sovereign appears to us in his lofty isolation, we should try to discover how it is that subjects are gradually, progressively, really and materially constituted through a multiplicity of organisms, forces, energies, materials, desires, thought etc. (p. 97)

Conversely, weak forms of structuration describe the ways in which educators produce, resist, or appropriate structures. The methodological implication that results from covert uses of power is that one must attempt to identify the extent to which educators are aware, cognizant, and conscious of the structures that mediate their micropolitical activity and the extent to which they are able to change them. Methodological attention to weak and strong forms of structuration, consequently, entails depicting whose interests are represented and how these interests are represented within the organization. Greater attention to how desires are fabricated would develop a *politics of subjectivity* that would redirect units of analysis away from the traditional emphasis on identity politics in educational micropolitics (May, 2005). Micropolitical researchers, consequently, should not hesitate to reveal how power operates to inculcate desires – indeed, to produce desires – for political gain.

Axiom 4. Micro- and macro-environments are better characterized as symbiotic rather than as autonomous arenas.

> It is a question of method: *the tracing should always be put back on the map.*
> This operation and the previous one are not at all symmetrical.

– Deleuze and Guattari, *A Thousand Plateaus*

Rather than understanding educational micropolitics as conflicts between juridical territories, which are often characterized as distinct arenas, what is needed is an understanding of the symbiotic, and often emergent, relations that develop between micro- and macro-environments. Rather than developing more structural frameworks to explain micropolitical activity, inquiries ought to map power relations that identify micro- and macro-assemblages produced within institutional channels (Deleuze & Guattari, 1987, p. 156). In other words, micropolitical research ought to map the flow of power that assembles legislative and cognitive spaces together.

A critical cartography, or what Deleuze and Guattari (1987) call a "rhizome," is a way to map the unconscious assembly from understanding political action emerging from collapsed territories. Desire production, then, identifies how educators develop and use "new" cognitive geographies that are delineated from the revised boundaries of previously determined educator territories. Mapping these kinds of policy and organizational "dances" will indicate how power is socially and spatially constituted and reconstituted. More importantly, mapping power relations will describe the terrain that structures educators' interests, including, for instance, the spatialization of gender (Massey, 1994), the spatialization of race (Gulson, 2006), the conflicting territories of language (Mehan, 2001), and the cognitive schizophrenia of organizational performances (Ball, 2003).

Conclusion: Repoliticizing Education Micropolitically

Identifying stealth forms of power in micropolitical analyses should, ironically, provide the conceptual clarity to proceed with more certainty in micropolitical inquiries. Switching focus away from macroterritorializing attempts to understand power that operates stealthily will help explain how schooling has persistently maintained the status quo. Put differently, micropolitical research into stealth forms of power will help explain the organizational reproduction of schooling for the last 100 years and the innumerable failed attempts at altering those structures.

More complete descriptions of stealth forms of power that operate in schools will eventually redirect discussions toward the actions of individuals and groups in schools. At this point, readers may assume that mapping power in the ways I have suggested will end any hope of political action in schools. To the contrary, mapping stealth forms of power, to my mind, reaffirms the importance of political action in schools. The idea that educators act unconsciously most of the time does not suggest that they must act that way. Clear descriptions about the ways stealth forms of power operate can be very instructive. Rather than assuming that poststructuralism denies political action, we could begin by discussing micropolitical action as a repoliticization of education from the poststructural position from which I argue (see also, Biesta, 1995; Youdell, 2006). From this, a "new" politic is born from which to address equality, and perhaps democratic, concerns in public schooling (May, 2007). However, such a politic is practiced *micropolitically*.

NOTES

[1] I recognize the important debate surrounding Arendt's feminism, particularly as it relates to women of colour, particularly black women (see, for instance, Allen, 1999). In general, I am aware of the violence perpetuated on women in some of the surrealist imagery I use to illustrate ideas about power. Given that the majority of teachers in the United States are white women, the illustrations of violence are apropos even as they are detestable. Thus, an entire level of analysis about how women teachers are implicated as both disciplinarians and the disciplined lies outside scope of this book, unfortunately.

[2] Ernst noted that *The Angel of Hearth and Home* was a response to the "defeat of the Republicans in Spain" and that he wished to depict fascism as "a kind of juggernaut which crushes and destroys all

that comes in its path" (as quoted in Stitch, 1990, p. 159). Deleuze and Guattari (1983, 1987) discussed fascism from the standpoint of the body, much like Ernst does in his depiction of an assembled and mutated creature.

[3]   The eye held an important role in surrealist imagery. Like contemporary references, the eye represented surveillance mechanisms in surrealist mythology. More important, the eye represented a window to subjectivity that is often lost in contemporary discussions about surveillance. Buñuel & Dalí (1929) used the eye in both ways in their movie *Un chien andalou*, only to violently destroy the symbol, and its meanings, at the end of the film. I use their violent image of cutting the eye in Chapter 6 as a way to represent my thinking about the politics of subjectivity for teachers.

[4]   An often overlooked and, in my opinion, important piece of Foucault's oeuvre was embedded within Dreyfus and Rabinow (1982). Foucault's emphasis on "carefully defined institutions" followed his discussion about how institutions act as contemporary and differentiated forms of state power (i.e., schools, hospitals, prisons, etc.).

[5]   The figure was adapted from Talbert, McLaughlin, and Rowan (1993).

[6]   I use the term "isomorphic" in its generally accepted use; i.e., "isomorphism" is a one-to-one mapping between an object and its purported property, identity, or function. I use the term to raise attention to the distinction between "core" interests or beliefs and interests or desires fabricated from power. As such, isomorphic interests are those interests mapped onto specific territories and territories demarcated from essentialized identities.

[7]   I am using the term "segmentation" as it is used in micropolitical analyses from Deleuze and Guattari (1987, pp. 208-231).

THE GEOMETRIES OF TEACHER ASSEMBLAGE

Methods and Methodology

We are segmented from all around and in every direction. The human being is a segmentary animal. Segmentarity is inherent to all the strata composing us. Dwelling, getting around, working, playing: life is spatially and socially segmented.

> – Deleuze and Guattari, *A Thousand Plateaus*

To enjoy soup requires a spoon, not a fork. Likewise, to understand a phenomenon requires the appropriate tools. However, the trick is not to pick the biggest spoon, the deepest bowl, or the most sophisticated statistical package, the trick is framing questions that are important to the investigator and to an intended audience and then identifying a systematic way to study them that will enlighten both the investigator and the audience – that is, to have your soup and eat it too.

This chapter comprises two major sections. First, I explain the design of the research, review specific details of the case (access, time, participants, interviews, documents, and so on), and describe how data were analyzed. In some instances, I reflect on specific methodological issues as they relate to the larger project in an effort to help readers understand how I was involved in the research. Second, I provide a contextual analysis, or map, of Delphi Elementary School, my case study setting. Thus, the second section of this chapter is the initial analysis of the case. In the language of the research, the second section of the chapter is the rhizomatic map whereupon the accountability war takes place. Deleuze and Guattari (1987) explain:

> The orchid deterritorializes by forming an image, a tracing of a wasp; but the wasp reterritorializes on that image. The wasp is nevertheless deterritorialized, becoming a piece in the orchid's reproductive apparatus. But it reterritorializes the orchid by transporting its pollen. Wasp and orchid, as heterogeneous elements, form a rhizome. It could be said that the orchid imitates the wasp, reproducing its image in a signifying fashion (mimesis, mimicry, lure, etc.) … At the same time, something else entirely is going on: not imitation at all but a capture of code, surplus value of code, an increase in valence, a veritable becoming, a becoming-wasp of the orchid and a becoming-orchid of the wasp. Each of these becomings brings about the deterritorialization of one term and the reterritorialization of the other; the two becomings interlink and form relays in a circulation of intensities pushing the deterritorialization ever further.

Here, teachers and accountability policy dance like wasps and orchids within particular spatial fields and flows.

METHODOLOGICAL APPROACH

Interpretative methodologies are appropriate ways to make sense of people's actions.[1] They aim to describe patterns and themes among actions and to understand the rich, socially constructed aspects of people's lives. Interpretative methodologies seek explanations of phenomena in all their complexity, not on average. They are not geared to measure constructs and compute indices of central tendency. Instead, they require personal involvement from a researcher who interprets patterns that are complex, interwoven, and resistant to essentializing measurements. Even though the needed understanding must be sought through sustained and systematic design, interpretative methods are not caught in the trap of "detached objectivity." Geertz (1973) helps here:

> I have never been impressed by the argument that, as complete objectivity is impossible ... (as, of course, it is) one might as well let one's sentiments run loose. As Robert Solow has remarked, that is like saying that as a perfectly aseptic environment is impossible, one might as well conduct surgery in a sewer. (p. 30)

The choice of interpretative methodologies – to study teachers' micropolitical semiotics as responses to increased surveillance of their work – is consistent with the choice made to analyze these responses as micropolitical practices within flows of disciplinary, economic, and professional power. Several considerations guided my thinking about how best to design a systematic study to understand this problem.

Method

A single case study was an ideal method for pursuing the goal of this project. The benefits of the case method arise from its intention to describe situations that do not have a clear set of outcomes. Its aim is to understand the intricate complexity of one case; as a consequence, the case is not helpful if the goal is to generalize findings across settings or populations. Authors have argued that there are multiple forms of generalizing in research (Becker, 1990). Thus, it is incumbent upon researchers to discuss what form they are talking about.

The most prevalent form of generalization is from a particular sample of individuals to some larger sample of people of which they are said to be representative. In this study, I am do not generalize in this way. Another form of generalization is from a particular setting that is claimed to be representative of other settings. Shulman (1997) called these two forms of generalization "generalizability across people" and "generalizability across situations" (p. 14). Again, I do not generalize these research findings across settings.

Yin (1989) argued that researchers also used a third type of generalization – generalization to theory or analytic generalization. This is the type of generalization that I am using. I believe that this study generalizes to a set of ideas about the political processes in schools and to a set of theoretical ideas about how micropolitical resistance and subjugation operate. Thus, to make my "case," I must sufficiently describe the events, people, and politics in such a way that readers can develop inferences between this work and their own experiences.[2]

This research is a case study of how panoptic power operates in schools and the corresponding micropolitical processes that occur in schools under surveillance. This study generalizes to a set of ideas about the political processes in schools. I have decided to pay close attention to teachers' involvement with these processes in order to discuss this facet of school life. In effect, this case study should generate and support a conceptual framework that may have heuristic value in similar settings. As noted above, Yin (1989) described this kind of generalization as a generalization to theory. Thus, the idea of processes may be generalized even though variations in conditions create variations in results (Becker, 1990).

Purpose and Design

I selected a single-case design because I wanted to describe, in detail, how teachers exercised power in a school. Indeed, a study of two (or more) schools might highlight the different aspects of school culture and offer glimpses into how school culture impacts teacher decision making. A comparative, multiple-case study would be an excellent way to establish that teachers are powerful across different contexts (e.g., urban versus rural schools), powerful in particular ways (e.g., gendered power, as in an all-girls school), or powerful in relation to particular aspects of school organization (e.g., high schools versus elementary schools).

However, initial descriptions of teachers' micropolitics emphasized the desire and enjoyment of teachers in cases where solving problems about teaching and learning problems formed the rationale for their micropolitics (Lortie, 1975; Moore-Johnson, 1990; Reed, 2000; Curry, Jaxon, Russell, Callahan, & Bicais, 2008). These studies suggested that teachers' intellectual pleasure about teaching and learning, rather than local aspects of school culture, formed the rationale for their micropolitics. And the literature had, for nearly 30 years, presented the argument that teachers would engage in micropolitics to alter school structures that they believed would maximize opportunities for these "intrinsic" rewards (Lortie, 1975; Reed, 2000; Kelchtermans, 2007). However, not all teachers' micropolitics were simply self-interested behavior aimed at accommodating, surviving, or conforming to the social and cultural values of the school (Blase, 1987b). My intent was to understand the philosophical aspects of teachers' political lives – not the sociological and anthropological aspects of community politics.

Thus, I was not interested in making the point that teachers "have power," that this power is negotiated, or that this power was a cultural construct and social contest.[3] Rather, this study describes and explains how teachers in one school exercised power based on their beliefs and desires about students' well-being.

Essentially, I wanted to understand how teachers resisted the surveillance of their work, and I wanted to observe how the accountability policy grafted onto teachers' thinking, perhaps colonizing their beliefs and assembling their desires. As will be noted, accountability policies did not differentiate between schools and their widely different school cultures. Accountability policies were designed to standardize teachers and render their cognitions more rigid. My goal was to document these subjugation attempts and to describe how teachers resisted this colonization.

Selection Criteria

The basis for selecting a single research site rested on being able to generalize to a theory that might be used in effective micropolitical resistance. I decided to focus on how teachers participated in these processes. That is, I describe the kinds of political actions teachers engage in and provide corresponding reasons, or logics, for these actions. Thus, important factors determined a suitable case for study. Delphi Elementary School (which is a pseudonym) was an ideal choice for this study because it demonstrated several characteristics needed for the study of teacher power.

First, finding a single school that implemented multiple curricular and assessment policies was a central consideration (Ball, 1997). As noted in Chapter 1, multiple curricular policies (1) increase teachers' accountability and the surveillance of their work and (2) raise doubts about the ability of teachers to make educational decisions for students. Therefore, a single case based on a school in the midst of implementing new policies allowed me the opportunity to describe how teachers exercised power in different ways, to explain how teachers identified with their professional decisions across a range of disciplinary intentions – indeed, a range of overcoding, disciplinary wills.

Second, the teachers at Delphi were under enormous pressure to improve state-mandated test scores. In this case, assessment policies were related to the implementation of curricular policies. Because Delphi had not performed well on state-mandated, standardized tests, the district mandated new curricula. And because Delphi had not performed well on new curricula, surveillance accompanied the school's performances: deterritorialization ↔ reterritorialization. Remember, the idea of surveillance, or the idea that power is structured into school activities, forms the entire theoretical commitment of this study. Thus, I needed to maximize the pressure of accountability in this study to understand how teachers exercised power in relation to this facet of school life. I also selected the school because it is situated in a state that is currently mandating state performance standards and aligning these standards to a high-stakes accountability test – the Washington Assessment of Student Learning (WASL). A school that is in a state that is well into the throes of high-stakes assessment and accountability is a prime candidate for studies on teacher power in the context of surveillance.

The third criterion centered on the issue of political conflict. Bacharach and Mundell (1993) argued that most studies of organizational politics neglect to describe the school "struggle" – what participants understand to be a conflict and the cause for their exercise of power. I wanted to avoid this methodological error. Delphi Elementary School was in the process of implementing eight different curricular and eight different assessment policies, which were mandated by the district and the state. This study, consequently, examines conflicts that erupted over the issue of who has legitimate knowledge about how best to educate students at Delphi Elementary. This struggle is related to the curricular and assessment policies that the district and state use to monitor teachers.

In Chapter 1, I argued that curricular and assessment policies are technologies designed to monitor teachers. These forms of surveillance erode teachers' professional identity by circumventing teachers' ideas about what is best for students. Ingersoll (2003) argued that the struggle over whom has legitimate knowledge about students' welfare is responsible for the shortage of teachers in the United States. Ingersoll rejected previous arguments that claimed that the teacher shortage in the United States was a product of enormous teacher retirements and/or student population increases. Rather, Ingersoll argued that large numbers of teachers leave the profession because schools and districts do not allow them to make formal or stated educational decisions in schools.

I selected an elementary school because the organizational structure is less bifurcated than secondary schools, which are often departmentalized along subject matter lines. By removing some of the variability in school structure, I could more easily identify how power circulated within the entire institution and how teachers exercised power differently within the same institutional structures.

Yin (1989) noted that a single case might have sub-cases "embedded" within it. This idea informed my approach. I selected an elementary school because it provided sub-cases of teachers and, therefore, sub-cases of how teachers exercised power within the school. For instance, by studying how an experienced and a novice teacher made sense of school politics and how they exercised power within the same structure, I was able to understand how teachers developed their micropolitical skills (Curry et al., 2008). Likewise, by contrasting teachers' experiences, rather than school environments or departmental structures, the research yielded insights into how teachers understand the political environment of the school. Hence, I was better able to understand the reasons for teachers' micropolitics. Additionally, comparing (and contrasting) sub-cases of teachers' exercise of power helped me to better understand how power circulated in the school (which helped me to develop a better understanding of the capillary nature of power).[4]

Finally, the selection of a single case heeded Yin's (1989) practical warning that "the conduct of a multiple-case study can require extensive resources and time beyond the means of a single student or independent research investigator" (p. 53).

DATA COLLECTION STRATEGIES AND EMERGENT ISSUES

Borrowing a Few Techniques

The selection of appropriate strategies to collect data was important to understanding the phenomena in question. Participant observations, interviews, and document analysis framed the techniques for data collection in this inquiry. While I have borrowed these techniques from anthropology, I do not believe this inquiry to be ethnographic, or what others have described as "critical ethnography" (Madison, 2005). The research did not entail the amount of time needed in the field that traditionally marks ethnography. A large amount of time is usually reserved in ethnographies so that the researcher may attend to several relevant problems in the broad context of the research (the idea being that the problem will be interpreted in relation to local culture).

That is not how I interpreted what I experienced. While this inquiry borrowed techniques from anthropology, my interpretative stance described teacher power in relation to teachers' beliefs and desires about teaching and learning and less in relation to aspects of school culture. I focused on (1) conditions of the accountability formation and (2) the effects of power on teachers. The research, then, can be characterized as policy archaeology and policy genealogy rather than an ascription of cultural attributes to teachers' decision making (Foucault, 1972, 1977; Gale, 2001; Scheurich, 1994).

That is not to say that there were no cultural aspects to how teachers conceive of and use power. In fact, further research in this area may compare and contrast the cultural aspects of teacher power among different schools (e.g., high versus low socio-economic status schools, predominately black versus white schools, male versus female schools, private versus public, and so on), as mentioned above. I envisage a long and hopefully productive research agenda of documenting and building a "library of cases" that could be compared and contrasted over time. As the battle over teachers' professional identity continues globally, I also imagine that moving this study into a longitudinal framework will help me and others to understand how states and districts respond to this pressure internationally and how micropolitics affect macropolitical change, if at all. However, I framed this research as a genealogy about teachers' deterritorialized knowledges and the corresponding micropolitical acts teachers use to reterritorialize their cognitions. Rather than simply documenting the cultural practices of educational conflict, I wanted to make a contribution to theory development that could be used in effective micropolitical resistance.

In the following sections, I describe my strategies for data collection and the specific details of the case. I do so for two reasons. First, I want to provide readers with critical information about the case. Second, I want to provide readers with a sense of who I am – that is, since I am the primary research instrument, I am obliged to provide some of my reflections about how I approached issues that emerged from the general methodological design I selected.

Access

Obtaining access to Delphi Elementary School was easier than I expected or, more precisely, feared. My initial visit to the school was set up through an insider – a friend of mine who taught at the school. Interestingly, Glesne (1999) suggested that one way to expedite access is "to know an insider who is familiar with the individuals and the politics involved who can advise you in making access decisions" (p. 39). I've always marveled at the fact that politics, and particularly micropolitics, is taken for granted in our day-to-day lives as something to be negotiated. I do not know if Glesne thought that obtaining access would provide anecdotal data for a study about micropolitics when she wrote that sentence. In many ways, the idea of obtaining access is not simply a particular method to be considered by interpretative researchers, it is a significant research topic within the study of micropolitics.

I worried for several days prior to this meeting – what reasons might a principal and faculty have to participate in a study designed to understand what, in my experience working in schools, was discussed only with small groups of faculty at local taverns after work? What if the principal denied my request? The clock was ticking. I decided that the best way to approach what I thought to be such a sensitive issue – power and politics – would be to not use those terms in my request for access. Instead, I framed my request around the central idea that teachers and principals are often stressed and/or pressured by the competing demands of curricular and assessment mandates. I, in turn, wanted to study how teachers and principals responded to those pressures.

My plan worked. In fact, the principal immediately discussed several related tensions created for or in the school by curricular and assessment mandates. To my surprise, she used the words "power" and "politics" frequently during our initial discussion. In a later conversation, she stated:

> I entered the principalship because I wanted to know where curricular decisions were being made. I knew that there was a big political part to it, and I really wanted to understand how curricular decisions get made in districts and in the legislature. I really wanted to understand how it all filters down to schools. I guess I just wanted to understand all that and more, and I was kind of starting it in my own classroom, and I thought, "Well, I want to see a bigger picture rather than just a grant for my classroom; I want to see how this all interconnects – who's in power." It's very complex, obviously.

My jaw dropped. As it turned out, she had just left teaching to assume the role of principal because she believed that this new position would allow her to better understand who makes the decisions about what is taught and how it is taught in schools. Similarly, she too was on a quest to understand the nature of teachers' professional identity.

Participants

I describe the participants as a group rather than as individuals. I do so for reasons of confidentiality. In instances where more detail is warranted, for instance in the sections where I present my findings, I offer more elaborate details about individuals. I present data anonymously when I believe that the participants' observations will put them at risk.

Five teachers and the principal selected themselves (self-selected) for the study during a faculty meeting in which I presented the study (with the help of the principal). Teachers taught kindergarten and the second, third, fifth, and sixth grades. The principal had taught Grade 5 prior to her appointment as school leader. Initially, I was disappointed that the fourth-grade teacher did not participate in the study. In this state, fourth-grade teachers administer the state exam in elementary schools, which increases the pressure of accountability for those teachers. However, as it turned out, the current fifth-grade teacher had been the school's fourth-grade teacher for the previous 4 years. He decided to move to the fifth grade because of the overwhelming amount of pressure he received as the result of the state exam. This is what I wanted. I wanted to understand how the state exam, in part, affected fourth-grade teachers. Because of his background, the fifth-grade teacher was a perfect fit for the study. In the end, I was pleased with the distribution of grade levels in the sample.

Teachers had varied working experiences. Teaching experience range from 2 to 25 years. The mean number of years teaching for all participants was 12. Four participants had taught at Delphi for 2 or more years. The principal and the kindergarten teacher had only begun working at Delphi that year. All participants were Caucasian, and 1 of only 2 males on the faculty participated – the fifth-grade teacher. The only other male teacher in the school was the phys. ed. teacher.

Table 1. Participants

Name	Grade	Yrs. teaching	Yrs. at Delphi	Gender	Age	Ethnicity
Sara	K	15	1	F	55	White
Julie	2	2	2	F	25	White
Claire	3	25	6	F	52	White
Wilson	5	7	7	M	34	White
Maya	6	7	3	F	30	White
Natasha	P	9	1	F	30	White

The professional backgrounds of these teachers indicated that they were classroom experts who used a variety of complex instructional strategies to help students learn. Participants worked with colleagues and displayed a degree of collegiality with peers. All participants were certificated in the state – some in more than one state. Participants were professional leaders, both in the school and in the district. The sixth-grade teacher was participating in an action research mathematics project with a local university. The third-grade teacher was a member of the International Reading Association and participated frequently in its national conferences. The second-grade teacher was the school's writing coordinator and participated in several national digital Listserv projects. The fifth-grade teacher served as the principal designee, a conditional position that would enable him to assume responsibility of the principalship if the principal were incapacitated or otherwise unable to fulfill her duties. Four participants had master's degrees.[5]

Finally, 5 participants had experiences working in at least two different schools. I sought participants who had experience working in varied organizations so they would have an informed understanding about school politics and teacher power from which to discuss their thoughts. However, 1 participant had only worked in one school, Delphi. This particular sub-case was extremely important, for it allowed for comparisons with other participants' experiences and formed the basis for claims about how she developed a sense of organizational politics.

Participant observation
In 1997 Harry Wolcott observed that everyone is a participant observer in some way. Thus, he argued that interpretative researchers need to define what it is they are looking at. The distinction between my everyday observations and my research-based observations rested on what I looked for. During nearly 50 hours of observation over the course of 11 weeks in the field, I recorded field notes of teacher micropolitics based on teachers' perceptions of classroom effectiveness.

My observations took place in both formal and informal settings. I observed teachers in faculty meetings, the faculty lounge, classrooms, hallways, assemblies, the cafeteria, and during a parent reading night. I also looked for patterns among teachers' actions that provided me with interpretations about how they respond to teaching and learning conflicts in schools. Many conflicts were the product of teacher assessments, which were derived from student assessments, and these conflicts were observed most readily in the classroom and related to the selection of curricula that teachers believed matched students' needs better than what was prescribed.

Classroom observations were the least effective strategy to collect primary data on the phenomenon. However, these observations did provide important data from which to confirm or disconfirm other data. Observations during faculty meetings were extremely beneficial, though. These observations helped me understand how participants negotiated complex policy issues with their peers. Additionally, faculty meetings provided me with a wealth of information about the school, the district, and the state. I was amazed at how much time was spent on management issues during these meetings. I called these long episodes "logistical thinking," as the faculty talked about how to best coordinate, assimilate, resist, mediate, incorporate, adjust, and fix multiple and competing policies from the district and the state.

The school had designed an implicit, or unconscious, line of inquiry about how to best coordinate the overwhelming number of curricular policies. This logistical thinking was designed to produce the most efficient way to deliver teaching lessons that aligned with the next lesson, the next assessment, the next grade level, the next iteration of standards, and so on. This kind of thinking was often demonstrated in faculty meetings when faculty deliberated on how to add and/or reduce new initiatives. One teacher, during a faculty meeting about the different skills embedded in the Iowa Test of Basic Skills (ITBS) and Washington Assessment of Student Learning (WASL), reflected on curricular breadth and depth dichotomies and exploded, "All we do is rush, rush, rush through! Do the kids learn something? Do they really know things? There just isn't enough time to cover everything!" The coupling of high-stakes tests with numerous curricula only encouraged participants to seek out more and more streamlined versions of teacher-directed instruction. Instead of developing a conscious line of investigation about the pedagogical and curricular opportunities of these policies, participants perceived policy mandates as the sword of Damocles. Participants were more concerned with how to make non-decisions and to self-censor their needs (Reed, 2000). Direct confrontation with the policy environment was, apparently, not a collective, conscious option.

I should note that my decision to observe participants created another surveillance mechanism for teachers. As the primary research instrument in the study, I became another panoptic technology in the school, and, as is the case in interpretative research, observations are always affected by the researcher's presence (Silverman, 2004). My attention to issues of power in the study led me to even ask teacher participants about my presence (see interview question 23, Appendix). Interestingly, my choice to observe teachers assembled me into a research tool, and I appreciated Foucault's thoughts about not being outside the discourse that I was researching.

Document analysis
I underestimated the amount of time that would be needed to pursue this strategy. Hundreds of pages were read (some scanned) and analyzed during the study. Documents included, but were not limited to, curricula (Success for All, Quest, Open Court, Great Body Shop, Cooperative Integrated Reading and Composition, 6 Trait Writing, Art, various science kits), assessments (State Assessment of Student Learning, Iowa Test of Basic Skills, District Reading Assessment Proficiency, District Reading Assessment, District Writing Assessment, various interim measures), flyers for professional development workshops, daily staff bulletins, meeting minutes, district bulletins, and so forth.

Documents were obtained and analyzed as they related to expectations for teachers. Expectations included (1) what to teach, (2) how to teach it, (3) student assessment objectives, and (4) teacher accountability goals. I created a matrix that included these categories for each major document. Matrices were then used to compare documents to each other and to develop the broad expectations that teachers needed to follow.[6] In cases where a matrix would not align with a specific document (e.g., meeting minutes), I developed summary sheets that highlighted important issues related to the study.

Semi-structured interviews

Participants were interviewed individually using a semi-structured interview format (see Appendix). Fifteen interviews were conducted, and they averaged 1.5 hours in length. Interviews were tape-recorded with permission, and the tapes were transcribed. Follow-up questions were asked when I needed to clarify information. In developing the interview protocol, I adopted the working assumptions that schools are political organizations and that teachers exercise power in schools (see Appendix).

In order to understand how teachers' political actions were related to their instructional beliefs, I framed questions around ideas of curricular conflicts (e.g., whole language versus phonics) and teacher and student assessment conflicts. I probed to understand how participants manage these conflicts (e.g., What did you teach? Why? Who evaluated you? How?). In order to understand how teachers' political actions were related to the school's organization, I framed questions around ideas of situations where conflicts would be manifest. I probed to understand how participants manage these areas. I avoided asking questions that involved the terms "politics," "political," or "power" during the earlier portion of the interview because these words could have suggested pejorative understandings of events and people. However, the last interview question directly asked participants to describe their impressions of these words.

The semi-structured nature of the interviews was enormously beneficial to me when I analyzed the data. Knowing when questions were asked helped me to locate answers in a timely fashion. The regular structure of the interviews helped me to pinpoint aspects of the data that I needed to verify once the transcripts were coded.

The interviews were the single most effective data collection strategy used in this study. However, their effectiveness developed over time. I noticed that all participants were somewhat restrained during the first half of the first interview. Answers seemed pat, routine, obvious. It was only in the second half of the interview that participants seemed to "awaken" and offered details that provided the gist of the findings. The question that brought about a significant change in participants' responses was, "Do teachers ever just go along with a curriculum decision they don't support? Why? What do they do?" At this point, participants (and I) realized that this study was designed around what Noddings (1986) described as research *for* teaching instead of simply research *on* teaching (p. 506):

> Educational research has been oddly uneducational and ... one reason for this may be the failure of researchers to engage in collaborative inquiry. There is a pragmatic side to this problem, of course, but from an ethical perspective, the difficulty may be identified as a failure to meet colleagues in genuine mutuality. Researchers have perhaps too often made persons (teachers and students) the objects of research. An alternative is to choose problems that interest and concern researchers, students, and teachers. (p. 506)

I believe that one reason participants developed enthusiasm during the interviews was that they realized that I was trying to understand a very real problem in *their* lives. At this point in the interviews, I also came to believe that participants discussed these issues to help themselves understand policy and power issues in their work. The interviews, consequently, reminded me of the implicit bias built into the research; that is, my desire to develop a theory of resistance for teachers to confront the deterritorialization of their knowledges.

However, my participation in their lives stopped there. Unfortunately, I maintained a researcher's distance that precluded me from advising, or otherwise helping, participants on these complex issues. I believe I held this stance based on the naïve assumption that I somehow might jeopardize participants' and my own credibility. In retrospect, I wish I had had more time and resources to extend this research into an investigation with several participants, including the principal, of the negotiation of district and state policies. I believe that there is rich potential to collaboratively investigate many important issues that arose from this case study – not to mention the important partnerships that could be developed over time. I could have easily developed action research projects that centered on policy issues with several participants.

Once participants (and I) understood the implicit focus of the interviews, there was little to stop them. In fact, each participant responded at some point during the interview that the discussion had been cathartic, needed, and important. They explicitly stated that understanding how teachers responded to policy mandates would help them to develop the kind of professional autonomy that marked their professional lives. They believed this was important work, and I had difficulty keeping the tape recorder stocked with tapes.[7]

Data analysis
According to Erickson (1986), to analyze interpretative data is to "generate empirical assertions, largely through induction" and to "establish an evidentiary warrant" for these assertions by systematically searching for disconfirming as well as confirming data (p. 146). I followed this advice and thoroughly read and re-read the transcripts accumulated from the interviews.

I first read each participant's transcript independently, searching for what Erickson (1986) called "patterns of generalization within a case" – key linkages that serve as analytic constructs among many examples of participants' actions and/or speech (p. 148). I then compared each set of analytic constructs and developed codes from which to re-examine the data. Observations and analyzed documents were used to reinforce and/or triangulate codes. After using additional readings of the data to reduce the number of categories, I sought disconfirming cases to further distil important analytic statements. The process was repeated (iterative process) until I was able to defend my propositional statements with supporting evidence.[8]

From these readings and from the research questions, I generated empirical assertions that withstood subsequent analysis of disconfirming cases. In order to establish the validity of the assertions, I excerpt the transcripts and present them so that the reader may follow the logic of the analysis. All quotations are actual data and presented in ways to illustrate the interpretations I make.

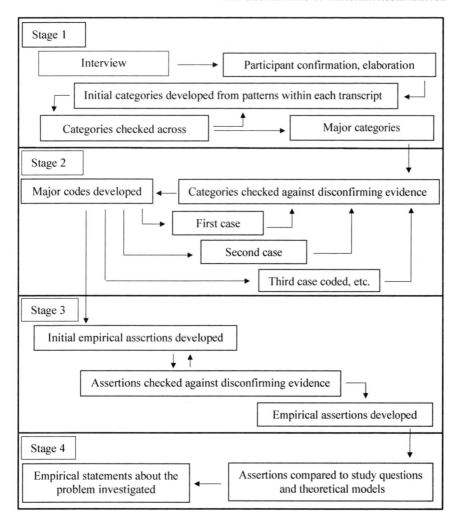

Figure 17. Method for coding interview transcripts.

SPACES OF TEACHER MICROPOLITCS: SEGMENTED, STRIATED, AND CODED TERRITORIES

"Just the facts" is what Sergeant Joe Friday, a fictional television detective, would say to informants during crime investigations.[9] And, with objectivity, cool logic, and a little luck, Joe Friday compiled the "facts" into a rational arrest. Sergeant Friday assumed that if informants would provide just the facts – not their thoughts about the facts – he would be able to interpret and analyze the information correctly so that he would discover the truth. Sergeant Friday believed that distinctions existed between the facts and interpretations, or analyses, of the facts. He believed that informants could detach themselves from what they had witnessed and simply report the facts of the case. For Joe, facts stand apart from meaning.

This section presents the first level of analysis. It describes and explains the setting, or context, of Delphi Elementary. However, unlike Joe Friday, I report facts with interpretation and analysis: this chapter reports a contextual analysis of Delphi's setting. Goodwin and Duranti (1992) remind researchers that the Latin root of context *(contextus)* means "a joining together" (p. 4). In context, participants and environments are joined together and interact with one another.

My analytic approach, then, differs from traditional empirical work – studies that report the context or setting in stark detail, devoid of meaning. Rather, I report the context as a set of interactions between participants and environments. This chapter, consequently, is essential to understand the analyses of teacher micropolitics that follow.

Philosophically, there is no distinction between the facts of the environment and an interpretation of these facts – the facts are what has been interpreted. The description of the context, then, was a constructed meaning between participants and myself and our segmented lives. At times I show some of these effects; at other times, I tell these effects. I wanted to avoid the problem that Clifford Geertz (1973) so eloquently relayed to other interpretative researchers:

> There is an Indian story – at least I heard it as an Indian story – about an Englishman who, having been told that the world rested on a platform which rested on the back of an elephant which rested in turn on the back of a turtle, asked … what did the turtle rest on? Another turtle. And that turtle? "Ah, Sahib, after that it is turtles all the way down." (p. 29)

I did not analyze the context of Delphi in terms of searching for the origins of events – the turtles so to speak; rather, the goal I set for myself was to "conceptualise the relevance of local happenings so that they relate to analytic issues; but simultaneously, [I] remain sensitive to how these reframings might distort the meaning of member categories" (Emerson, Fretz, & Shaw, 1995, p. 174). Goodwin and Duranti (1992) suggested that researchers take "as a point of departure for the analysis of context the perspective of the participants whose behaviour is being analysed" (p. 4). The perspective I elicit is the subjugation of teachers through the context of their work.

Cartographical Caveats

A word of caution. The study of power is essentially a study of interactions and constructed meanings. Schools do not exist in vacuums: schools reside in complex environments, environments that often demand and mandate much of what occurs inside them. Delphi Elementary is no exception. The contextual environment is crucial to understanding how teacher participants exercised power and were subjugated by power.

Throughout this chapter I use the terms "context," "context effects," and "contextual interactions" as a way to describe the complex, and complicated, district and/or state environments of Delphi Elementary. I borrow definitions from Talbert, McLaughlin, and Rowan (1993) to help me explain these terms:

> We use the term context to mean any of the diverse and multiple environments or conditions that intersect with the work of teachers and teaching – such as the school, subject area, department, district, higher education, business alliance, professional networks, state policies, community demographics. The notion of context effect implies the influence of particular context conditions – values, beliefs, norms, policies, structures, resources, and processes – on teaching practice and, in turn, students' educational outcomes. (p. 46)

Sometimes I use the term "contextual interactions" as a synonym for "context effects."

I begin by discussing the immediate district and school environments, including demographic data, social class information, and the current building (structural and architectural) conditions. I then describe the state and district assessment policies and pause to report on how Delphi performed on the assessments. Keep in mind that I have theorized that these assessments act as panoptic technologies to evaluate teachers and schools. Although the study took place in 2001, I report demographic data from 1991 to 2006 to help readers understand spatial flows and territorial segmentations over a period of time.

Finally, I describe the context of Delphi in a linear fashion for the purposes of telling this story; however, my experiences studying this school and district reinforce the idea that rationality and order were illusions.

SPATIAL DEMOGRAPHICS, ECONOMIC FLOWS, AND POLITICAL TERRITORIES

> What ... is a flow? It is belief or desire (the two aspects of every assemblage): a flow is always of belief and desire. Beliefs and desires are the basis of every society, because they are flows and as such are "quantifiable"; they are veritable social Quantities, whereas sensations are qualitative and representations are simple resultants ... Hence the importance of statistics, providing it concerns itself with the cutting edges and not only with the "stationary" zone of representations.

> – Deleuze and Guattari, *A Thousand Plateaus*

Delphi Elementary School is surrounded by the city. Two busy interstates and two major airports border the school. On a clear day, observers can catch a glimpse of the downtown skyscrapers that silhouette one of the 25th largest cities in the United States (US census).

The district enrolled over 17,000 students in 2001, and Delphi enrolled 360 of those students in Grades K-6 during that year. The district monitors 18 elementary schools, 4 middle schools, 12 high schools, and 2 vocational/alternative schools. In the last 15 years, the district has seen rapid changes in its student demographics, even though the total student population has remained relatively constant. In 2006, the district had 2.5 times as many students eligible for free or reduced lunch than it did in 1991. This suggests that the average family income in the area has dropped substantially, while other Americans have benefited during this same 15-year period of economic expansion.

One reason for the economic decline in the area is the new runway being built by one of the airports. The property values of this area have plummeted as the airport gobbles up residential space and transforms it into runway space. Interestingly, though, the airports are also the major employers of the area. This presents a major conflict for local residents and has become a lively topic for local political debate. On the one hand, the airports provide residents opportunities for employment and low-income families opportunities for home ownership. On the other hand, the airports have significantly reduced the quality of life for long-time residents. The decline in property values, coupled with an increase in air and noise pollution, contributed to the financial decline of the area. The new runway has become a political symbol of this debate. Bumper stickers and political lawn signs dotted the landscape, stating the ideological preferences of residents. The most immediate impact for the district, which became a subject for political debate, was the constant micromigration of students in or out of the district. The district averages a 28% mobility rate among its students and families each year.

Another important change in the district is that the student of colour population had tripled in the last 15 years, bringing with it lower family incomes. Students of colour made up 63% of the district student population in 2006. Additionally, students who speak English as a second language (ESL) represented a total of 54 separate languages in the district.

These demographic numbers suggest that white, English-speaking families emigrated at a rate nearly equal to the immigration rate of students of colour and ESL students. Additionally, based on increased free and reduced lunch participation, families who immigrated into the district had fewer financial resources than families leaving the district. These statements are based on the fact that the entire district student population has remained relatively constant over 15 years, even as significant demographic (ethnic and economic) changes have occurred within the total student population. The student population is no longer ethnically or economically the same as it was 15 years ago. Even with these migration patterns, English-speaking students remain the majority, even though white students, as a whole, are now the minority.

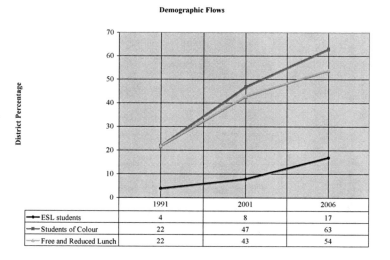

Figure 18. Demographic flows (1991-2006).

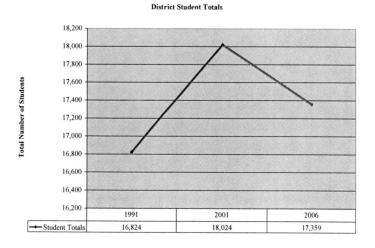

Figure 19. District enrolment (1991-2006).

School Demographics

Delphi's student population in 2001 slightly exaggerated the district's demographics during the same time period. Fifty-six percent of Delphi's students

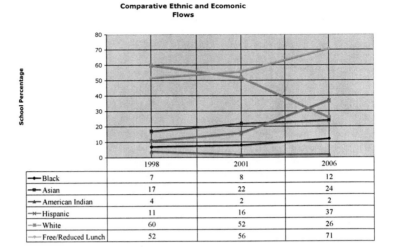

Figure 20. Ethnic and economic flows at Delphi (1998-2006).

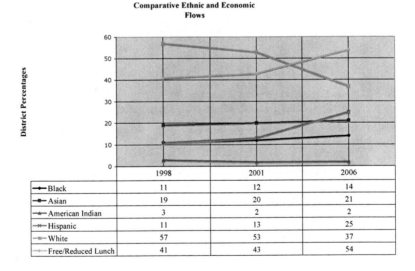

Figure 21. Ethnic and economic flows – District (1998-2006)

were eligible for free and reduced lunches. Of the 360 students, 8% were black, 22% were Asian, 2% were American Indian, 16% were Hispanic, and 52% were white. Compared to the district at large, Delphi enrolled greater numbers of white students and students eligible for free or reduced lunches. Over the past 15 years, Hispanics were the fastest growing group at Delphi, and whites were the fastest declining group at the school. A high mobility rate (27%) further characterized the students and their families at Delphi. Ninety-seven students did not begin or end their schooling at Delphi in 2001, even though these scores were included in accountability decisions.

SCHOOL ARCHITECTURE: SEGMENTED AND CODED MICROPOLITICAL SPACES

Built in 1954, Delphi is housed in a building designed to last 20 years. The building contained 13 K-6 classrooms, 2 ESL classrooms, a music classroom, a library, a computer lab, 2 paraprofessional tutoring classrooms ("para"), a speech therapist/counselor room, and a special education classroom. The school contained a boiler room, kitchen, gymnasium that serves double duty as a cafeteria, faculty lounge, faculty storage-supply room and office, nurse's room, and principal's office.[10]

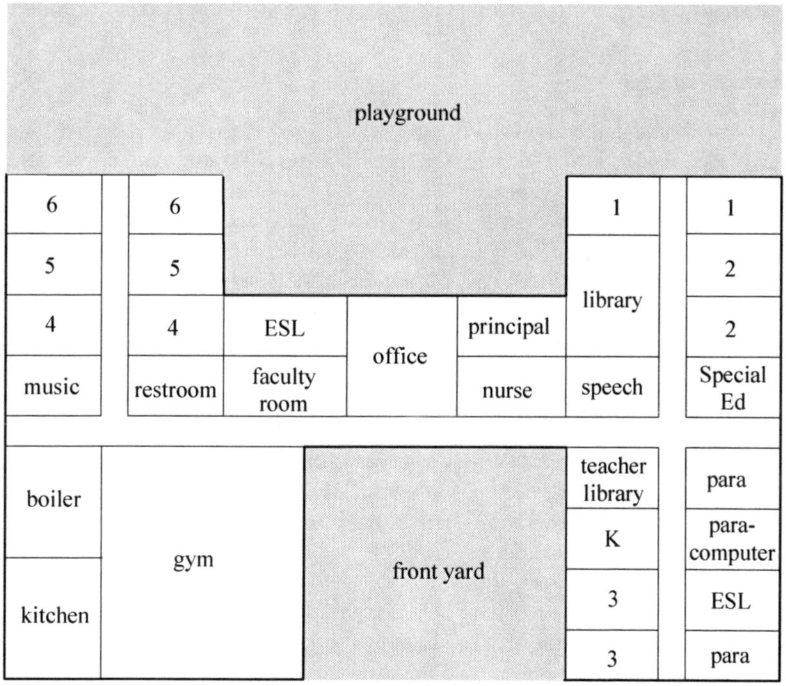

Figure 22. Delphi architecture, 2001.

During my time at Delphi, the building constantly demonstrated how it labored to keep up with the wear of time. Buckets littered the school floor to catch rainwater that dripped through a porous roof. Small rivulets trickled down walls, collecting into sizeable streams that flowed down sloping hallways. For 2 weeks, a damaged water main, next to the gymnasium, was being repaired. The ruptured pipe did not catch everyone off guard, though. Two participants chuckled about how they had relayed information about a "growing bump" in the gym floor to the district. Participants reported the bump when children dangerously, and in some cases humorously, tripped over it during relay races in phys. ed.

Concerned faculty also discussed the level of mold in the building. During a faculty meeting, a new teacher requested that the district conduct a survey of the amount of mold in her room because she believed it caused her nose to clog first thing in the morning. She explained that as soon as she entered her room, her breathing became labored and her nose became stuffy. Experienced teacher participants at Delphi noted that the building had a history of mold, and, only 2.5 years ago, toxic levels of mold were found in some classrooms, including the new teachers' room.[11] Later, when I expressed my concerns about the building during one of my visits, a teacher told me that a leaky roof, broken pipes, and mold are manageable nuisances compared to the instance when a sewer line broke underneath the playground and students mistook the bubbling puddle for mud.

Contextual Implications

I report the dilapidated conditions of Delphi because effective teaching and student learning are compromised during the pitter patter of rain *in* classrooms. This compromise exacerbates the already difficult job of teaching.[12] However, that is an easy claim to make. In a district that is losing financial resources steadily, it is apparent that the problem of building maintenance is becoming more and more critical. Whose responsibility is it to guarantee that Delphi is structurally sound? Whose responsibility is it to secure a comfortable place where teachers and students can achieve accountability demands? Are teachers responsible for building maintenance?

Even innovative curricula and policies are doomed to fail if building conditions are so poor that students and teachers must constantly adjust buckets to catch the trajectory of falling rainwater. Worse yet, very little effective teaching and learning will take place in schools where people feel sick. Poor building conditions sent a clear message to one participant: "If it's a crummy school atmosphere, you feel crummy, and you feel like you're being treated that way." As I will show, these dilapidated school conditions are not discussed when test scores, used to assess teachers and schools, are reported. This is a wholly unfair practice. Evaluations of student learning and pedagogy need to be conducted in buildings that support teaching and learning, not undermine the process.

Finally, readers should note the cellular structure of the building. Lortie (1975) commented that the "egg crate school" maintained teachers in isolated roles within the school (p. 14). Lortie argued that "schools were organized around teacher separation rather than teacher interdependence" (p. 14). The idea of teacher separation as a result of building architecture is particularly important in this study for two reasons. First, the cellular structure of Delphi resembles the panoptic architecture that "assured the automatic functioning of power" (Foucault, 1977, p. 201). The cellular structure of Delphi reinforced how power was structured into the school by separating teacher participants. Foucault reminded us that the cellular structure of organizations, the separation of people, essentially makes people feel that they are under constant surveillance:

> All that is needed then is to place a supervisor in a central tower and to shut up in each cell a madman, a patient, a condemned man, a worker, or a school boy ... Hence the major effect of the Panopticon [is] to induce in the inmate a state of conscious and permanent visibility that assures the automatic functioning of power. So to arrange things that the surveillance is permanent in its effects, even if it is discontinuous in its action [generates] that the inmates should be caught up in a power situation of which they are themselves the bearers. (pp. 200-201)

Second, teacher separation, as a result of the building architecture, produced isolated micropolitics rather than collective action. I devote the next chapter to an explicit defense of this statement. At this point in the analysis, readers should take note that the exercise of power is embedded in the physical design, the cellular structure, of the school.

ACCOUNTABILITY POLICIES: ABSTRACT WAR MACHINES OF OVERCODING

Building decay is not the only thing that assailing Delphi. The school is under pressure to improve both their Washington Assessment of Student Learning (WASL) scores and their Iowa Test of Basic Skills (ITBS) scores. The State Assessment System comprises three broad programs: statewide standardized testing, classroom-based assessments, and staff development. The statewide testing program focuses on the Essential Academic Learning Requirements (EALRs), the state's content standards. The EALRs provide achievement indicators for the state, districts, schools, and individual students.

State Technologies of Deterritorialization

The WASL and ITBS are standardized tests that report achievement data for individual students, schools, districts, and the state. This information is used by the state to monitor and evaluate school and district performances. The WASL is a series of criterion-reference tests in reading, writing, listening, and mathematics. These standards-based assessments incorporate three item types: selected response (multiple choice), short constructed response, and extended constructed response. The ITBS is the norm-referenced component of the statewide program. This measure collects achievement information about the basic skills that provide the problem-solving skills found in the EALRs. The ITBS is used to provide independent evidence to validate the WASL assessments, while providing policy-makers comparisons between state achievement levels and that of the nation and most other states; in other words, it constitutes a de facto nation-wide network of education surveillance in the United States. The WASL and ITBS are panoptic technologies; that is, surveillance techniques used by the district and state to assess teachers and schools.

Accountability Sanctions – Disciplining Threats and Coercive Terror

Schools that achieve a 3-year average of less than 25% improvement in their students' ability to meet mathematics standards on the WASL (40% for reading) are subject to any or all of the following conditions:

– withholding of state and district funds
– reconstitution of school and/or district personnel
– removal of particular schools from district jurisdiction
– appointment of a state trustee to manage the school and/or district
– abolition of the school and/or district
– authorizing student transfers

Delphi underperformed relative to the district averages on the WASL. Eight-five percent of Delphi's fourth-grade students were below the WASL mathematics standard, and 87% were below the state WASL writing standard in 2001. Of the 18 schools that contain Grade 4 in the district, Delphi placed in the bottom 15% for math scores and the bottom 15% for writing scores. From 1997 to 2001, Delphi had not met the standard on the WASL mathematics portion of the test. As a consequence, Delphi is eligible for any of the proposed state interventions listed above. Delphi fared better on the 1999 ITBS test, in which it met or surpassed the state requirements in mathematics and reading.

District Technologies of Deterritorialization

The state funded district development of additional classroom-based assessments as long as they were tied to the EALRs. In district elementary schools, six measures, depending on grade level, were used to additionally monitor teachers and intensify the gaze. These measures included three interim measures (reading, math, and writing), District Reading Assessment Proficiency (DRAP), District Writing Assessment (DWA), and a District Reading Assessment (DRA). DRAP is administered five times, over 6 months, in Grades 2 through 6. The interim measures for reading, mathematics, and writing are administered three times a year for Grades 1 through 6. The interim measures are loosely defined: sometimes they are scores from existing measures (e.g., DRAP), and sometimes they are additional assessment measures from mandated curricula. For Grade 2, the DRA is administered once a year in addition to other measures. For Grade 4, the DWA is administered once a year in addition to other measures. All told, district elementary students and teachers were assessed 3 to 10 times a year, depending on grade level and subject matter.

Table 2. Testing schedule for elementary schools in the district.

Grade	District assessments: *Interim Measures*	Frequency (per year)	State
K	Reading, math, writing	3	
1	Reading, math, writing	3	
2	Reading, math, writing	2-3	DRA
	DRAP	5	
	ITBS	1	
3	Reading, math, writing	2-3	ITBS
	DRAP	5	
4	Reading, math, writing	2-3	WASL
	DRAP	5	
	DWA	1	
5	Reading, math, writing	2-3	
	DRAP	5	
	ITBS	1	
6	Reading, math, writing	2-3	ITBS
	DRAP	5	

Note: State tests are given once a year. DRAP = District Reading Assessment Proficiency; ITBS = Iowa Test of Basic Skills; DRA = District Reading Assessment; DWA = District Writing Assessment; WASL = State Assessment of Student Learning.

Professional Development as District Apparatus for Subjectivity Colonization

The final component of the system is a staff development program that "trains" classroom teachers and principals in assessment practices.[13] The district has a contract with a local professional development agency that "delivers educational services that can be more efficiently or economically" taught. This agency offers nine courses for district teachers, six that are aimed at aligning instruction with the WASL. A quick review of four course titles reinforced the importance of the WASL in the district:

– Raising WASL Scores
– Your Curriculum – Classroom Assessment and WASL
– From 7th to 10th Grade WASL: What Lies Between?
– It's Coming – The 8th Grade Science WASL

If the importance of the WASL was not found in the title of the professional development courses, it was found in the description of the courses. For instance, two professional development courses that emphasized teacher accountability claimed to help teachers to (1) "learn how to use question specific [mathematical] scoring rubrics similar to the ones on the 7th to 10th grade WASL" (Y2 Assess in Mathematics) and (2) "focus on the traits of good writing as assess [*sic*] on the

WASL. Participants will practice applying typical WASL-like prompts and the scoring criteria to their classroom curriculum and assessments" (The Write Stuff).

Cafeteria-style professional development models have economic benefits for the school districts that employ them. However, these models are essentially aimed at providing teachers with the skills of generic pedagogy – pedagogy that does not take into account specific student needs in classrooms (Little, 1989; Loucks-Horsley, Hewson, Love, & Stiles, 1998). As a result, a participant in the study made this observation about the effectiveness of the professional development model: "It's interesting going to a math workshop because it turns into a grilling session for the poor people putting on the workshop. The presenters just get ripped on when they don't talk about teachers' kids and classrooms."

Curricular Policies: Overcoded Knowledges for Cognitive Deterritorialization

Delphi implemented, or continued to implement, eight different curricula that were mandated by the district. The curricula that Delphi implemented were as follows:

- Success for All (SFA – reading)
- Cooperative Integrated Reading and Composition (CIRC – an extension of SFA)
- Open Court (reading)
- Quest (mathematics)
- Six Traits (writing)
- Great Body Shop (health)
- Science (district kits)
- Adventures in Art (art)

Delphi Elementary is situated in a complex policy environment, an environment that regulates and monitors the operation of schools through a web of panoptic technologies. The district is experiencing rapid changes to its student demographics and to its financial resources. However, tests, by themselves, do not improve student learning. Tests only indicate where problems lie, and, to compound matters, these problems are debatable. Participants were skeptical about the validity and reliability of the measures. Wilson summed up participants' doubts:

> I guess if I were working at Technology Island [a wealthier school district], I'd feel great about test scores. The district's actually come out and said, "If you want to improve your scores in the WASL, switch districts." I had a buddy who did. Fourth-grade teacher, and she has no problems. The WASL is not even a concern for her. She knows the kids are going to do well because they have the support at home. They have together lives. They have together parents. Family life means so much to children that academics are going to fall in place much more easily for wealthier families. My friend said, "She was amazed." She said, "It was great." She had most of her kids pass the WASL. They did really well. But it's not the same for us. [We have a]

different client base – ESL and huge turnover. But I'm sure she patted herself on the back for it.

One reason I selected Delphi for study was the consistently low test scores that the school reported on the WASL. However, and contrary to popular selection techniques, I did not assume that these scores necessarily reflected poor teaching or poor school leadership. Rather, I believed that Delphi's low test scores were positively correlated with the economically disadvantaged students enrolled in the school (Anyon, 1997). However, poverty only made the job of teaching more difficult. Students at Delphi were capable of an excellent education in the hands of competent and caring teachers. However, the question about how to do this was compounded by the level of poverty at the school. Curriculum standards and standard assessments that do not account for students' economic disadvantages can further marginalize students while simultaneously increasing pressure for teachers to meet these standards.

Regardless of why students at Delphi were not meeting standards, there is a difference between identifying problems and solving them. Only in the hands of skilled, knowledgeable, and determined teachers will students achieve the kinds of academic gains expected; this will not be achieved through repeated assessments and/or frequent shifts in curricular policy. This is why we have teachers. Maya, a participant, carefully, but with a touch of sarcasm, stated: "It'd be nice if we could just hand the state standards to the kids and say, 'Read this, there'll be a test at the end of the year. Have any questions? Ask me.' Teaching doesn't work that way." However, in response to low performance, the district engineered a series of assessment, curricula, and professional development policies that assembled teachers' subjectivities into strategic micropoliticians and surrogates of government control.

NOTES

[1]   I use the term "interpretative" to refer to this family of research methodologies. I want to try to avoid defining this inquiry in opposition to quantitative methodologies. In fact, I use a fair amount of basic descriptive statistics in this chapter to substantiate several points.

[2]   Bassey (1981) has observed,

> An important criterion for judging the merit of a case study is the extent to which the details are sufficient and appropriate for a teacher working in a similar situation to relate his [sic] decision-making to that described in the case study. The relatability of a case study is more important than its generalizability (p. 85, as quoted in Bell, 1999).

[3]   As, of course, it is. The point here is that I framed the research as a policy archaeology/policy genealogy rather than as a cultural phenomenon.

[4]   For the remainder of this study, I refer to the specific school district that Delphi is situated in as "the district." Similarly, I refer to the specific state that Delphi is located in as "the state." I use these terms deliberately to protect participants' confidentiality and because participants rarely, if ever, referred to the school district by its name. Participants referred to the school district by pronouncing the acronym of the district name in a phonetic way – a kind of local speech practice that took me a while to decipher. It would be very difficult to reproduce textually without belying confidentiality. Finally, I selected these particular terms for rhetorical purposes related to the study. My use of the

anonymous terms "district" and "state" is designed to provide readers with a sense of the monolithic entities these bureaucracies represented to participants. This will become clearer to readers in subsequent chapters, particularly the one that follows.

[5] Sara developed a brain tumor and passed away after the study completed.

[6] That is, the expectations of district, state, and professional curriculum developers.

[7] In trying to understand participants' "developed enthusiasm" during the interviews, I became persuaded by McCracken's (1988) important observations on the benefits afforded to participants during qualitative interviewing:

> The qualitative interview gives the respondent the opportunity to engage in an unusual form of sociality. Suddenly, they find themselves in the presence of the perfect conversational partner, someone who is prepared to forsake his or her own "turns" in the conversation and listen eagerly to anything the respondent has to say. This characteristic of the qualitative interview leads to other benefits, including the opportunity to make oneself the center of another's attention, to state a case that is otherwise unheard, to engage in an intellectually challenging process of self-scrutiny, and even to experience a kind of catharsis. (pp. 27-28)

[8] Adapted from Portin (1995).

[9] The television show was titled *Dragnet*.

[10] The structure described here was razed, rebuilt, and re-opened in 2008.

[11] In 2007 the librarian filed an "occupational hazard" lawsuit against the state regarding mold in the building. The case is still pending.

[12] Sarason (1982) and Shulman (1997) believe the job is "impossible" in dry classrooms (Sarason, p. 152; Shulman, p. 497).

[13] I have retained the original language of the assessment policy in this description. The word "train" signals a belief about teachers' professional identity – that is, teachers are likened to dogs. Changing teachers' pedagogy will only come about when people change the way they think about teachers.

INSURRECTIONS OF SUBJUGATED KNOWLEDGES

> An entire thematic to the effect that it is not theory but life that matters, not knowledge but reality, not books but money etc.; but it also seems to me that over and above, and arising out of this thematic, there is something else to which we are witness, and which we might describe as an *insurrection of subjugated knowledges.*
>
> – Foucault, *Power/knowledge*

If the previous chapter described the rules of the game, this chapter describes how teachers played the game. It explains teachers' resistance to deterritorializing attempts and, more importantly, describes the justifications for their resistance to policy. In other words, this chapter provides readers with a description about how teachers practiced micropolitics and an understanding of why they practiced them.

Teacher participants resisted policy to better meet students' emotional and academic needs. This finding contradicts previous research that described teachers' micropolitics as self-interested behavior. Clearly, teachers were implicated in their micropolitical behavior. However, the basis for their exercise of power rested on their intentions for student learning rather than on acquiring political capital only for themselves. Thus, teachers' micropolitics are better understood as *insurrections of subjugated knowledges* within larger attempts to improve student learning. Foucault (1980b) explained the idea of subjugated knowledges and how such knowledges act as a form of political resistance:

> By subjugated knowledges one should understand ... a whole set of knowledges that have been disqualified as inadequate to their task or insufficiently elaborated: naïve knowledges, located low down on the hierarchy, beneath the required level of cognition or scientificity ... It is through the re-emergence of these low-ranking knowledges, these unqualified, even directly disqualified knowledges ... which involve what I would call a popular knowledge (le savior des gens) though it is far from being a general commonsense knowledge, but is on the contrary a particular, local, regional knowledge, a differential knowledge incapable of unanimity and which owes its force only to the harshness with which it is opposed by everything surrounding it – that it is through the re-appearance of this knowledge, of these local popular knowledges, these disqualified knowledges, that criticism performs its work. (p. 82)

The chapter proceeds by describing how teacher participants modified or resisted curricular policy to better attend to students' welfare. At Delphi, curricular policy was so generic, and poorly coordinated, that it often failed teachers in their particular contexts. Heaping more and more policy onto participants only enhanced their feelings of inadequacy and guilt.

Participants' resistance to policy was based on their autonomous beliefs and desires about teaching and learning. These beliefs about students formed the basis for teachers' nomadic journeys (diagnoses and decisions) within deterritorialized knowledge landscapes. Teachers' beliefs were not self-interested behavior because the desired intent was to assist students (i.e., others). However, the fact that teachers' rarely shared their reasons for resistance reinforced their lonely nomadism. Consequently, teachers' isolated nomadic journeys generated school conflicts if teachers held conflicting knowledge passports. To compound matters, nomadic conflicts were exacerbated by how participants practiced micropolitics.

CURRICULAR POLICY INSURRECTIONS

Participants resisted and/or modified district curricula to better serve students. This was their exercise of power. In the midst of 16 separate curricular policies, participants spoke about the need to modify, adjust, change, alter, resist, or delete curricula that did not benefit students. For instance, curricula directed participants to teach lessons on topics that students had already mastered. Conversely, curricula would detail lessons that required knowledge that had not yet been covered in class. Teachers resisted the policy sequence despite the stiflingly panoptic assessments that monitored their performances and levied judgments about who they were as teachers.

Figure 23 illustrates participants' shared thoughts about their responsibilities to mediate and/or resist curricular policies. Two participants, Sara and Claire, used similar phrases to express their reasons for curricular resistance. Figure 23 situates Sara's and Claire's statements as a heading under which substantiating statements by other participants are placed. Teachers resisted or brokered rather than implemented policies. Participants did not fit the mold of a technician, parceling out bits of work in regimented ways assigned by others. I often asked participants how they managed to mediate all of the curricula they were given. I was stunned at the thinking required to synthesize the many competing knowledges and then arrange these knowledges into some coherent form for students. Participants, interestingly, considered my questions about "curriculum management" naïve. For them, resisting, revising, arranging, brokering, mediating, and shaping policies was simply part and parcel of the day's work. Instead, participants answered my questions about curriculum management with questions of their own that asked me why the district mandated so many policies. "Why are they doing *this* to us?"

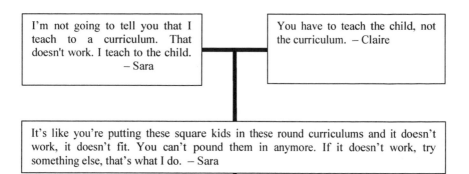

I'm not going to tell you that I teach to a curriculum. That doesn't work. I teach to the child.
– Sara

You have to teach the child, not the curriculum. – Claire

It's like you're putting these square kids in these round curriculums and it doesn't work, it doesn't fit. You can't pound them in anymore. If it doesn't work, try something else, that's what I do. – Sara

You just can't say well, here's the book and we're going to follow this, this, and this. If it's not going to work for the kids, then I'll say, "Okay, we're going to do something different." For instance, we're supposed to start at the beginning of the year doing reading groups where they had reading books that they would take home. Well, it's way too soon, way too soon. So it was, like, "Why would I do that? The kids are not ready." So you have to modify the curriculum to work for the kids.
– Claire

I have a lot of freedom, I do. If [the assessment] doesn't really fit as well as it should, then it's not going to work for the kids. My ideas are ideas for the kids, not for the WASL and not for the administration. I'm teaching the student, and if I am assessing a child on an assessment form that is not appropriate for the children that I'm teaching, I won't use that. I'll find another assessment.
– Julie

If I don't truly believe what we're teaching, then I will subvert it and change it. When the doors are closed they're going to see something different than when the doors are open. So if I truly don't believe in what I'm teaching, or what I'm being told to teach, then I'm not doing it. I'm putting on – I'm doing two sets of lesson plans. Kind of like keeping two sets of books: you have the set of books for the auditors, and then you have the set of books that you're really doing your stuff. I think teaching is like that, in that, if you truly don't buy into what the curriculum is telling you to do, you are going to subvert it to some degree.
– Wilson

Figure 23. Teachers' insurrections to curricular policy.

79

My questions about curriculum management were difficult for teachers to answer because underneath such questions lay issues of subjugation, teacher quality, and individual politics that are anathema in the egalitarian world of education. The principal, however, answered questions about curriculum management with disdain and anger:

> I don't care what curriculum you're using, it's good teachers that really make the difference. And sometimes the focus on all these curricula, it's like if a teacher's good at teaching reading, you're going to probably teach reading pretty well. But right now there's such a shortage of good teachers that the focus is what curriculum can support anyone in teaching.

The national teacher shortage had trickled its way down to the district (Ingersoll & Smith, 2003). Instead of investing in teaching learning or transferring curricular control to teachers (Ingersoll, 2003), the district spent enormous resources on curricula and surveillance to control teachers. Given participants' steady exercise of power within consistently shifting deterritorialization attempts, I imagined a perpetual conflict of accountability   resistance in the district. This conflict, I supposed, would be very profitable for curriculum developers, test makers, and teacher educators.

INSURRECTIONS OF SUBJUGATED KNOWLEDGES

Throughout this chapter, I unearth and apply Aristotelian knowledges to teachers' talk. Readers can find Aristotle's discussion about many of these knowledges in his *Nicomachean Ethics*. My application of Aristotelian knowledges is designed to act rhetorically rather than as a definitive guide to teachers' cognitions (or as a guide to Aristotle for that matter). My use of Aristotelian knowledges identifies teachers' endemic knowledges used to insurrect curricular policy, and my use of these knowledges accentuates the idea that these endemic knowledges were archaic in the Foucauldian sense of "naïve" and "disqualified." I imagine scholars of Aristotle will find my usage unbearably thin. Fair enough. My concern, however, is to illustrate how teachers relied on other knowledges instead of the ones embedded in policies that were deterritorializing their subjectivities. These archaic knowledges were the political weapons used to surmount reterritorialization attempts.

The most recurring theme that supported teachers' micropolitics was their corresponding intention, belief, and desire to attend to student welfare. In these cases, participants invoked a knowledge known as *phronesis* to disrupt curricular mandates. *Insurrections of phronesis* – diagnostic thinking (Korthagen & Kessels, 1999) or practical judgment (Coulter & Wiens, 2002) – were discretionary decisions that were extremely beneficial for students when teachers' judgments were correct. Figure 24 displays participants' testimony about why they made discretionary decisions about student welfare. I have figured data in this way to provide readers with a sense of a "school voice" about notions of phronesis – a sense that individual participants shared similar ideas about their professional identity, although they rarely organized as a collective counterforce in the school.

I take time out because of the children that are here. Some of their home backgrounds are awful, and some of them have been in some traumatic events. Others have extreme anger problems, so I'm sorry, but [teaching] has to wait a few minutes while we get calmed down and go through what we value and what we don't. I mean Quest [the math curriculum] can say you have to be this far and this far and this far, but man, you have to work with what you've got. If they're not ready for it, they're not ready for it.   – Claire

In my reading group, we're supposed to get through the story in 5 days. Well, because I have 10 who don't speak English well, there's no way I can get through it in 5 days. It takes me longer. Which means I can't cover as much curriculum. I'm trying to do it more in depth so they really get it and not just zoom over it.

– Sara

In any curriculum, there's a lot of gaps in vocabulary, especially for the ESL kids, which I have six of this year. I had no ESL kids last year, so that's been something that's geared me toward what . . . I teach and how I present it.

– Julie

If the kids are in a mood where they just cannot work with one another, then you choose a route around that. So, if I plan for a group activity and I decide that day that they cannot handle it, we'll do one-on-one, or something like that.

– Maya

We have to absorb and deal with children's lives that aren't always pleasant, and it rips us up. You have to be able to understand that this kid has problems, and we're going to do the best we can with them. But you can't heal everybody, and you do the best you can and get them as far as you can while you have them.

– Wilson

I have 14 children in my reading group, and 10 come from homes where they do not speak English. And some of them will get grounded if they speak English at home because of other family members. They don't want to offend them by speaking English because the other person doesn't speak English. So they actually get in trouble if they speak English at home. Well, I can't be totally successful at teaching them our curriculum if the only English they get is at school.   – Claire

Figure 24. Teachers' insurrections of phronesis.

81

Participants spoke at length about students who spoke English as a second language. These students needed additional time, attention, and curricular adaptations to better attend to their academic achievement. Also, students from low-income families needed emotional comfort and emotional security before learning could take place. Emotional and physical abuse, alcoholism, divorce, and truancy marked some of the pedagogical terrain participants traversed. Participants described some of these nomadic encounters as unpleasant and traumatic. The numerous relocations that low-income students and families experienced further characterized the macroflows teachers traversed.

In addition to phronesis, participants' micropolitics were informed by macroknowledge wars about teaching and learning. These macrowars were waged on teachers' *episteme*, scientific knowledges, and were evidenced at Delphi as (1) phonics versus whole language debates and (2) mathematical computation versus conceptual development debates. For instance, Julie explained her reasons for resisting a reading curriculum:

> Open Court [curriculum] is more phonic-oriented, and some of us felt that phonics didn't necessarily apply once children got past that – some kids don't need that. And [the district] presents it as well, "Every kid needs phonics every grade no matter what." Well, when you can ask children, "How do you chunk those words and what's this sound" – if you can have them do it, you don't need to teach it. At least that's my view on it.

Once participants identified students' academic needs, they responded to curricular mandates according to their beliefs about teaching and learning. In this particular example, Julie's curricular resistance is defined by what she perceived would benefit the student. This is a different explanation of teachers' professional identity than is offered in previous studies that explain the exercise of power among teachers as being motivated for selfish reasons (Blase, 1987b). Julie's talk (above) also demonstrated the macroknowledge landscape wars that participants traversed within the school. Indeed, participants' micropolitics were practiced in relation to these broader macropolitical knowledge wars: macropolitics micropolitics. As Deleuze and Guattari (1987) reminded us, "Everything is political, but every politics is simultaneously a *macropolitics* and a *micropolitics*" (p. 213).[1]

The finding that teachers resisted curricular policy to better attend to students' academic and emotional needs resonates with earlier studies about teacher power (Greenfield, 1991; Lortie, 1975; Moore-Johnson, 1990; Reed, 2000). And, like these earlier studies, teacher phronesis was a source of intellectual pleasure for participants. However, insurrections of phronesis were performed as autonomous acts of resistance. At the microlevel, the insurrection of subjugated knowledges was a lonely, chaotic, and nomadic war. Consequently, the exercise of power among teachers was idiosyncratic, contributing to serious doubts about their capacity to be collectively accountable. The term "idiosyncrasy" acts pejoratively in education, rather than signaling promise or potential as in so many other professional fields. My use of the term is meant to signal the potential of teachers' discretion within micropolitical coalitions and allies.

Individual and idiosyncratic insurrections were also based on additional knowledges that participants used. It is in these cases that teachers' micropolitics can be understood as insurrections of naïve and disqualified knowledges.

The Re-Emergence of Naïve and Disqualified Knowledges: Genealogical Memories

[Microphysics of power] are not univocal; they define innumerable points of confrontation, focuses of instability, each of which has its own risks of conflict, of struggles, and of an at least temporary inversion of the power relations.

– Foucault, *Discipline and Punish*

When I asked participants to explain the basis of their professional decisions, they often paused and asked me to repeat the question. I did. I asked the question in a variety of ways; for instance, "Explain how you determine what students need? How do you know (what students need/what to do)? Why did you teach that lesson (instead of that lesson)? What informed your thinking about that decision?" I was searching for the reasons that supported their insurrections, for the reasons for their resistance. Participants often chuckled to themselves, reclined in their seats, rubbed their faces, and/or looked to the ceiling. Our talk about their political resistance was difficult, taboo, and filled with feelings of anger, guilt, and fear of punishment. I had opened a dangerous conversational space.

To illustrate the complex area of participants' beliefs and their impact on their micropolitics, I present microportraitures of each participant. The portraits take the form of interview transcripts so readers may follow the complexities of these interactions and my involvement in walking with teachers in this dangerous frontier. Readers may benefit from reviewing participants' demographic information to understand how grade level and experience impacted the exercise of power among participants. I continue to use Aristotelian knowledges as a way to identify the endemic and archaic knowledges that teachers used to resist policy. Transcripts have been edited to make reading easier.

Claire – Insurrection of hypolepsis and episteme

Claire, who taught for over 25 years, based her policy resistance on knowledge obtained from participating in the International Reading Association (IRA). Claire indicated that she uses *hypolepsis* – generalized or conjectural knowledge of reading – to make pedagogical decisions that differed from those given to her by policy. It may be the case that Claire is invoking episteme, or scientific knowledge, in her talk. The distinction rests with understanding the macro-reading wars and the extent to which knowledge about how to teach reading is something that is codifiable.

Claire talked about her professional decision making as being in response to the cacophony of advice peers and district administrators gave her when she asked about what to teach. In her statements, readers will catch a glimpse of how knowledge deterritorialization produces teacher schizophrenia, which is embodied in different discourses about how to teach.

> *Claire:* It takes so much time to prepare district curricula, and how valuable is it really? Some people say, "They're not being tested on the WASL right now," and other people are saying, "Forget the science, do the writing, spend your time on writing, reading, and math." And then some people say, "Drop that." Others say, "No, you need to do this because it's informational writing." All I hear is, "Do this, no, back off, you can't do that – you don't have time to do that." Who do you listen to?

> *TW: [Pause]* Who do you listen to?

> *Claire:* My background. My background was being a Title One reading teacher for about 20 years in Michigan. I had my master's in elementary reading instruction from Michigan State. And I've been to lots of . . . I've been to two International Reading Association conventions, one in Texas, one in Canada. I've been to over 15 years' worth of the Michigan State ones, which is one of the best in the whole country. The convention [is] every year for 4 or 5 days, and it's absolutely out of this world. Top people from all over the world, Australia, everywhere. So I have a pretty good background in [knowing how to teach] reading.

The cacophony of policy "voices" telling Claire what to teach are all sublimated in relation to her own experiences learning in professional organizations. Her affiliation with the International Reading Association (IRA) formed the basis of her decision making in the content area of reading. The IRA is a national organization that is highly influential in the development of reading education policy in the United States. When she discussed her reasons for exercising power, Claire reflected on her own education at Michigan State, her participation in the IRA, and her own knowledge developed from years of experience working with students. It is the affiliation with these organizations that Claire allied herself with and which formed the foundation for her micropolitics.

The schizophrenia associated with the deterritorialization of teachers' knowledge is acutely present in Claire's talk. In this sub-case, Claire is able to ventriloquate the macropolitical deterritorialization of teachers quite well. "Who do you listen to?" is not just a phrase that pointed to the cacophony of macropolicy-makers, it was pointed directly at Claire's very own subjectivity regarding her right to reterritorialize her work in meaningful ways. Interestingly, Claire's reterritorialization was focused only on the reading curriculum. Consequently, Claire's ellipses regarding other curricula suggested that she held multiple discussions within herself about ways to reterritorialize other knowledges in her teaching. It would be difficult to distinguish these schizophrenic discussions from how Claire thought about reterritorializing herself. Thus, Claire's hypolepsis and epistemes were subjugated knowledges that directed her reading of curricular insurgencies and produced her professional schizophrenia.

Wilson – Insurrections of doxa and techne

Wilson exercised power to meet the needs of – what he considered to be – two types of learners: linear and non-linear thinkers. In a related manner, Wilson believed that most curricula were designed sequentially (as curriculum narratives). Thus, Wilson believed that the purpose of his micropolitics was to help students learn from both a linear and non-linear perspective, which for him meant disrupting the mandated policy sequence when necessary. Wilson's beliefs about people-types and curriculum-types (and inherent matches between the two) were predicated on a form of knowledge that Aristotle described as *doxa*, or opinion. Wilson's curricular insurrections were based on the subjugated knowledge of doxa.

Wilson's insurrections were further predicated on his technical-scientific view of curricula. As a consequence, Wilson's micropolitics were based on the additional knowledge, *techne,* or skill for production. The technical-scientific curriculum was made famous in the Tyler model and is a rational model of curriculum that uses a means-end way of presenting subject matter. Scholars often critique this model as being a "factory" model of curriculum development (Pinar, Reynolds, Slattery, & Taubman, 1995).

Wilson mediated linear curricula when he believed students would not benefit from a deductive approach to learning (and vice versa). Wilson believed that this dichotomy (linear versus non-linear) also characterized teachers. For Wilson, then, the exercise of power was the alignment of student learning styles with teacher pedagogical styles in negotiation over school narratives and knowledge sequences. Consequently, the term "techne," as used by Wilson, refers to subjugated (and antiquated) knowledge that tailors the curriculum to the student. Hence, Wilson's understanding of techne is different than the neo-techne required of educators today in which they follow curricular scripts lockstep or suffer punishment.

> *Wilson:* Let's take for example the Quest curriculum. The Quest curriculum is heavy into the conceptual basis of mathematics, but it doesn't provide the child with any real algorithms to deal with. Children are expected to pretty much come up with their own algorithms, "How did you do this problem? How did you solve this problem?" Some kids don't work that way. [If] you're a real linear thinker, you say, "Give me the method, give me the algorithm to do this multiplication problem."

> *TW:* And that's from the district, or principal, or ...?

> *Wilson:* There are student-learning styles that I acknowledge. Let's say this person has a particular learning style, but I don't think we've done much research into the concept of teaching style. And [curricula] are designed ... they're always designed for linear teachers. For those of us who aren't as linear, it's more difficult to follow the linear format. Instead, I say,

"Okay, this is the information, the objectives that you want to convey."
But give me the objectives, and I'll get there the way I get there with my
stories and my anecdotes. I do more of that kind of teaching and
activities. I try different learning styles because it's hard to do just the
linear deal for me.

TW: So, do you design your own lessons?

Wilson: For instance, I spent [time] on this [lesson] where kids crashed on the
test that was this particular health curriculum. They got to a point where I
said, "Okay, three people passed, three people got the over 80%, wad up
your papers in the recycle bin; we're not going to be using this test for
your grades." Unfortunately, it was important stuff about personal safety
issues and emotions, and so I went back over this stuff. I talked about it
some more, and that's where maybe your teaching style doesn't match as
well with their learning styles, and you try and figure out another way to
get to them. But I was pretty much following the rules, and it didn't work.

TW: So, students may need differences in how they're taught to get some of
this material.

Wilson: I try to cover it from both ways. I try to do the linear thing as well as
my more sporadic stuff.

The significance of Wilson's knowledge – doxa – rested on the fact that his
pedagogical beliefs remained unexamined rather than simply being wrong. This is
an important distinction when invoking doxa instead of other "verifiable" forms of
knowledge (e.g., episteme). Voluminous literatures exist on ideas about student-
learning types, critiques of rational curriculum development, and pedagogical
styles. Wilson might have benefited from any number of development activities
designed to investigate the important questions that he raised. These activities
might take the form of investigating the nature of mathematical learning rather than
learning about how to implement curricula, for example. Unfortunately, Wilson
taught in a district that provided professional development activities designed to
"help" teachers adhere to state testing and district curriculum implementation
rather than support teacher learning.

The deterritorialization of teachers' knowledges left little time for Wilson to
examine his suppositions. Hence, the deterritorialized machine of accountability
created a vessel out of Wilson to carry out the curriculum mandate. However,
Wilson's micropolitics were evidenced in his failure to meet scheduled assessment
deadlines, even though, in this example, he completed the curriculum tasks. He
was quite adamant that student learning come before the completion of timely
assessments for use by the accountability machine. In this case, Wilson's
micropolitics temporarily thwarted the external accountability system when Wilson

used the assessment for classroom practice rather than for external accountability desires.

Sara – Insurrections of doxa

Sara also relied on doxa for her micropolitics. Sara believed that students were naturally curious and that teachers should meet interests that emerged from their students' curiosity. As a consequence of this belief, Sara, more than any other participant, understood curricular and assessment policies as "suggestive guides" rather than as specific mandates to be followed. Her use of the word "freedom" is a critical sign about her conception of teacher power. She understood teacher power as a micro*freedom* to revise or resist the curriculum.

> *Sara:* You always have to extend. My whole philosophy is I teach to the highest level of the class, and I will extend all of them. Now, of course, there are some that are not going to get it as well as others, but that's okay. You'll come back to it, and you'll come back to them in some other way, and you have to have that freedom to do that with certain kids. I have a child in the afternoon class, absolutely gifted, very immature, and I can let her wander around the room because I cannot make her sit in one place, she cannot follow the norm. She can't fit in that box everybody else does, and that's okay. I may have a little notebook up there or something else that she is working on. I'll have something that she can do.

> *TW:* That gives me a good idea of some of the pressures … *[interrupted]*

> *Sara:* I'm teaching to the highest level; students will always have extra, and they will extend themselves. Ninety-nine percent of the kids will extend themselves naturally. If they finish with something, they can go over to the alphabet board, and they can be making words.

Sara's micropolitics are rooted in her opinion that students are naturally curious. Thus, Sara understood her job to be to identify a "zone" of classroom learning that resulted from the diversity of classroom curiosity. After Sara identified a learning zone, students followed their natural curiosity in independent ways, à la Rousseau's *Emile*. Taken out of context, this kind of pedagogical reasoning could have disastrous results for students who do not know how to participate in activities that have little or no instruction. However, the key word that Sara repeats in her testimony is "extends." Sara uses this word three times in her testimony to identify the times when students used her classroom instruction as a springboard into additional independent activities she designed to facilitate their learning.

However, this idea of classroom learning requires Sara to keep careful tabs on student learning. Again, a golden opportunity existed for the district to shift its curricular policy in ways that would assist Sara to develop independent assessment practices. Instead, the district policies were geared toward standardized assessments that Sara had to resist daily through her curricular micropolitics.

CHAPTER 4

Subjugated Knowledges Revisited

Participants' beliefs about teaching and learning formed a strong basis for their eventual exercise of power. At this point, only Claire explained how she developed her beliefs about teaching and learning – through professional organizations. Wilson and Sara did not explain how they developed their ideas about how students learn; for example, linearly or through natural extension. As a consequence, Wilson's and Sara's knowledges remain unexamined and characterized as opinion, doxa, or unverified ideas (but possibly verified). Nevertheless, Wilson and Sara exercised power according to these beliefs about how students learn.

This raises an important question in the study of teacher micropolitics: How do unexamined teacher beliefs impact classroom instruction? The significance of this question rests upon the fact that teachers may entertain any number of racist or sexist beliefs about students (Webb, 2001). Since teachers exercise power in schools, what kinds of activities should teachers participate in to help them examine their beliefs so that they may exercise their power in responsible (i.e., legal, moral, professional) ways? How might curricular policy act in this way?

The next two portraits reveal normative activities that produced archaic and disqualified knowledges about teaching and learning. The first portrait illustrates sustained inquiry about one's practice. In this case, Maya participated in an action research project that helped her develop evidence for her curricular resistance. In this portrait, her political resistance was substantiated through study. The final portrait suggests important considerations that teacher education might address when helping novice teachers investigate their beliefs about teaching within accountability machines.

Maya – Insurrections of emperia and nous
Maya is the only participant who systematically investigated her practice. Maya participated in an action research project to help her better understand how to teach mathematics, specifically skills involved with mathematical problem solving. Maya believed that this project helped her to understand her practice and her students and that it provided opportunities for micropolitical collaboration.

The importance of action research should not be overlooked as a way to help teachers systematically examine their beliefs about teaching and learning. The first benefit of such an approach is that the process allows teachers to tailor their investigation to their immediate classroom situation. This is not professional development aimed at generic skill acquisition; rather, this type of learning allows teachers to directly address the individual students in the classroom by systematically examining their beliefs about students, learning, and curricular content. More important, it helps them to act on their decisions. As noted earlier, participants found pleasure in this aspect of their work. This process might have helped Wilson and Sara examine their implicit ideas about student learning.

TW: What did you base your decision on about how to teach problem solving?

Maya: My action research question about how to teach my kids to problem-solve independently.

TW: Action research ...?

Maya: Action research is a way teachers reflect about their own practice and ask questions about things they can change about the way they teach. They ask a burning question that is going on in their classroom or with their own teaching.

TW: How are you doing that?

Maya: I was chosen [by the principal] to be one of these people as part of the sixth-grade pilot program, where they wanted sixth-grade teachers to really focus on math this year. So they could change the way math is being taught in the district. I meet with other sixth-grade teachers and this woman from [a local university], and we've all developed questions about our math practice. We read a lot of research about teachers and our ... and the questions we have. Now we are trying to find answers, collect data, to our questions.

TW: How does this process help you?

Maya: Well, for a couple reasons. The action research helps because it makes me more aware of my teaching. By asking my question, sure I could ask it and go along my daily life, but by doing action research, I ask that question about problem solving, so that's been my main focus this year. I know my kids have grown tremendously in their abilities to problem-solve independently. One reason I know that is because on our last problem-solving class, I noticed that other teachers are about where I was in October in terms of this whole problem solving in math communication. Work they brought in was where my kids were in October, and I was very aware of that. The work I brought in showed that my kids were much more sophisticated with problem solving. This was the first time I realized, "Wow, my kids are really getting this." It was very clear to see the growth they had and that I had as a teacher in terms of how to teach this effectively. The other thing that has been so beneficial is not just reflecting about your practice and sort of focusing on that one question, but we're also getting [a] chance to meet with teachers in our grade level. This has been extremely beneficial because we are all able to share what we've gotten or how we've learned to teach this material effectively. For example, there's one teacher that I got this whole great idea from about how to teach fractions. That ability to share with colleagues has been beneficial. Also, these classes we take with these professors who are teaching us math concepts has also been great because it makes you feel more confident about the decisions you make about what you're teaching. We're looking across the Quest [math] curriculum, which is often confusing. We're finding ways to teach that makes more sense to us [our particular setting and context].

Another benefit of Maya's inquiry was that she had a grounded idea of student achievement. Maya's knowledge about her students' performances was immediate, substantial, and evidentiary. Maya's assessment of students was based upon their performance of the material (not on a constructed test question), and she documented their performance. As a consequence, Maya made curricular adaptations quickly and with precision. Her case demonstrates that teacher knowledge can be an incredible tool to meet students' needs. Waiting for standardized test scores may take months, and the scores will be subject to interpretation because of their constructed nature. Finally, Maya's explicit discussion about her collegial interactions is another benefit of her teacher research. Having allies was an important part of Maya's learning and something that she enjoyed doing.

Julie – Insurrections of mneme and doxa
In the final portrait, Julie reflected on her teacher education program. She remembered that what guided her decision-making process was the knowledges she developed in her pre-service program. Here, Julie's memory-knowledge, or *mneme*, surfaced during our discussions about her micropolitics. In this portrait, there is evidence that antiquated knowledges were taught and learned in teacher education programs. This occurred when professors of her method courses asked Julie to develop her own lesson plans. This placed Julie in a bind when the state and district assumed that teachers were technicians who needed to follow prescribed curricula that were tied to high-stakes tests. Julie understood this bind to be rooted in her teacher education, not in district and state regulations. The role of teacher education, then, is a major archaeological source of teacher knowledges. Teacher education produced naïve knowledges that implicitly contributed to the micropolitics of schooling when accountability machines deterritorialized these knowledges.

TW: What do you base your decisions on, for instance, why did you decide to teach [the idea] "compare and contrast," which was not in the curriculum.

Julie: [Irritated.] Because it was on the ITBS, and that's why.

TW: So the test had a lot to do with … I see, okay.

Julie: Yeah that … and, yeah, I'd say that would be it.

TW: But earlier you said that your teacher ed. program – or maybe I'm mistaken. Was there anything in your teacher ed. program that made you think about teaching something that's not in the curricula?

Julie: I think that's a lot of it. I think I really had a strong teacher ed. program, and I feel like I was really prepared to come into teaching. However, I don't want to go back to school because they pushed making up your own stuff. I have a binder that's full of math lessons that me and everyone in my class had to make up for every area that you would ever teach in math.

TW: In your methods course?

Julie: Yeah. They pushed spontaneity for me. My teacher ed. program was really geared toward that type of thing.

TW: And you like that or you don't?

Julie: I liked it when I was there. I don't want to go back to school for my master's because of it, because I know that I'm given all this stuff, and I don't need to make my own stuff. I think this is what got me into spontaneity. We had to make lesson plans for each area so we could go in and student teach in any area and be ready and prepared to do it. We would turn in our copy of it, and then she would copy it off, or we would copy it off for the whole class. We got whole class lesson plans for every single lesson plan that people wrote.

TW: So you have 20, 30 lesson plans …

Julie: And I've never looked at this since I started teaching.

TW: Because …

Julie: Every instructor presented it as making up your own things, and no one presented it as "you're going to have this curriculum, this curriculum, and this curriculum." You're going to have tons more materials than you ever want, could imagine. No one even presented it like that in teacher ed. and in student teaching.

TW: And would that have been helpful for you now that you're 2 years into it?

Julie: The last two classes that I had, Four Blocks, were really helpful because they presented a model. Not a curriculum, but a model. And I've used a lot of it, and I feel very, very grateful for that aspect of it. But the other classes were kind of "make up your own."

Julie was conflicted about the relevance of her knowledges, mneme and doxa, imparted to her in her pre-service program. At Delphi, so many curricula are mandated that Julie wonders why her teacher-education courses stressed lesson-plan making. As Julie noted, it is already done for teachers – and in ways that the state and district desire. As a result, the requisite knowledges to create lesson plans are antiquated, naïve, and disqualified. Student-tailored curricula were a waste of time in the new regime of accountability truth. As a result, Julie did not want to return for graduate education.

Importantly, Julie noted that creating lesson plans pressed her subjectivity toward notions of *spontaneity* and *making up your own*. This autonomous and learned freedom created a problem for Julie within regimes of power designed to subjugate such freedoms. Julie is conflicted; she is not sure what to base her exercise of power on – district mandates or the knowledges gleaned from her teacher-education program. Her micropolitics lacked conceptual clarity; her beliefs about teaching were stretched thinly across test content, curricular mandates, and the knowledges mneme and doxa gleaned from her pre-service education. Julie's cognitive nomadism, then, traverses bifurcated spaces of teacher knowledge that are deterritorialized from accountability machines. In this sense, Julie was also professionally schizophrenic.

School Schizophrenia

We should abandon a whole tradition that allows us to imagine that knowledge can exist only where the power relations are suspended and that knowledge can develop only outside its injunctions, its demands and its interests ... We should admit rather that power produces knowledge (and not simply by encouraging it because it serves power or by applying it because it is useful); that power and knowledge directly imply one another; that there is no power relation without the correlative constitution of a field of knowledge, nor any knowledge that does not presuppose and constitute at the same time power relations. These "power-knowledge relations" are to be analysed, therefore, not on the basis of a subject of knowledge who is or is not free in relation to the power system, but, on the contrary, the subject who knows, the objects to be known and the modalities of knowledge must be regarded as so many effects of these fundamental implications of power-knowledge and their historical transformations.

– Foucault, *Discipline and Punish*

Participants' micropolitics were based on archaeological knowledges developed in a variety of ways. Participants' antiquated knowledges were subsumed beneath the regime of accountability truth and were used to temporarily resist policy. Max Ernst developed a series of paintings that represented how landscapes encroach on archaeological ruins and the ephemeral creatures that inhabit these new landscapes.

In this study, it would be in error to characterize teachers' idiosyncratic knowledges as unaccountable or irresponsible. Teachers' micropolitics did not entail the enforcement and regulation of low student expectations. Participants' local meanings of accountability (responsibility to student learning and the students' families) created power-knowledge relations at Delphi. Moreover, participants' local meanings of accountability were intentional (albeit individual) and clashed with district and state accountability machines. While these subjugated knowledges left teachers schizophrenic, these knowledges formed the basis of their persistent and, at times, pleasurable micropolitics, which were determined to help students succeed.

Teachers' reterritorializations produced a school schizophrenia. Several participants entertained multiple voices concerning power-knowledge relations.

Figure 25. Max Ernst. The whole city. 1933. © Estate of Max Ernst / SODRAC (2008)

Other participants entertained absent voices as they sought justifications for their political acts. Participants' commitments to students, commitments neglected by accountability machines, acted as a press for micropolitical justification. At times, teachers' ethical stance about the condition of students was sufficient justification for their micropolitical acts. Teachers were nomads who sought clarity about their work and their micropolitics. However, teachers rarely formed nomadic "tribes," even when they shared archaic knowledges and these individual commitments left them schizophrenic within deterritorialized cognitive geographies. As one participant put it,

> Another thing that I found happening in my classroom is, the more they [the district and the state] emphasize something that I don't believe in, the more I try to accommodate. I almost become ... I almost become paralyzed and become ineffectual. I'm teaching something I don't agree with. I'm being forced to teach it in a certain way. I don't feel like it's doing anything. I'm trying to do the other one, but you're trying to do it in a way that's not drawing the attention of the administrators too much, and it becomes paralyzing. You find yourself wallowing instead of teaching. And, so, the kids become the real losers with the teachers who aren't buying in or working with what they're doing.

Participants' segmented cognitions provided evidence of their knowledge deterritorializations. Even Maya, who systematically investigated her practice, stated, "I am becoming more and more teacher-directed every day, and this is not what teaching should be." At Delphi, new and multiple identities were emerging within deterritorialized subjectivities, and some teachers were well aware of their own transmogrifications. Teacher power, acting against accountability power, created emergent and mutative identities within overgrown and neglected knowledge landscapes.

THE AESTHETICS OF SUBJUGATION

Curriculum policy, then, disqualified teacher knowledge in situ by amplifying the ambiguity – the situatedness – of these naïve and conflicting knowledges. Policy mutated teacher knowledge from knowledge in situ to knowledge *in politicus*. "Problems of practice" were immediately disqualified from the province of participants and reconstructed as political problems. Who now has the legitimacy (authority, sovereignty) to re-solve teaching and learning problems? How (what methods) shall teaching and learning problems be re-solved (i.e., recast in the "new" regime of performance)? Curriculum policy, then, was a system of paranoid or suspicious accountability aimed at regulating the perceived idiosyncrasies of teacher knowledge; indeed, it raised such craft knowledge up to the level of science. Policy aimed to eliminate the event-structured nature of contextual knowledge – "a whole set of knowledges that have been disqualified as inadequate to their task or insufficiently elaborated: naïve knowledges" (Foucault, 1980b, p. 82).

Teacher guilt, doubt, and confusion were effects born out of exterritorialization, a form of cognitive and epistemic violence. The goal of exterritorialization was not simply to subjugate the teacher – even if this, in a palpable sense, is what was occurring – but rather to "retool her" into a more effective instrument in education production (Fraser, 1989, p. 24). Policy schemes designed to surveil teacher knowledge were to create more productive and efficient teachers by linking them together into a disciplined, standardized, and productive knowledge: "to produce bodies that are docile and capable" (Foucault, 1977, p. 294). Policy was both dominating and producing.

Exterritorialization simultaneously deterritorialized teachers' knowledge. Indeed, this was the point. Performance standards and high-stakes tests were panoptic mechanisms that attempted to hold teachers accountable to "standardized" knowledge. Event-structured teacher cognition was no longer required; indeed, such knowledge was doubted, scorned, ridiculed, and attacked within the new discourse of performance. Within systems that sought to exterritorialize teachers' knowledge, Ball (2003) noted that teacher "beliefs are no longer important – it is output that counts. Beliefs are part of an older, increasingly displaced discourse" (p. 223).

Exterritorialization was not simply about displaying teacher knowledge in, and for, the public. Strategically, exterritorialization preyed on the reflections, uncertainties, dialogues, and the situatedness of teacher diagnoses. Exterritorialization simultaneously deterritorialized situated cognition into rigid knowledges for subsequent transmission throughout the school. By design, deterritorialization created new cognitive geographies delineated from the revised boundaries of previously determined educator territory. In effect, teachers' professional knowledge landscapes were rezoned (Clandinin & Connelly, 1996).

Teacher knowledge was decontextualized from teachers' communities, schools, classrooms, selves, and their relationship with students, and it was reterritorialized or re-assembled into quantifiable commodities – it was hard-scienced or "machinic effected" (Deleuze & Guattari, 1987, p. 333). Teacher knowledge was simply (very simply) assembled, commodified, and contrasted within media and other networks of education control (governments, school boards, real estate associations, PTAs, etc). Delphi was not an experiential learning lab but a streamlined site of production evaluated by its outputs, which could be assessed scientifically. Deleuze and Guattari (1987) described, in their own way, both the process and product of deterritorialization:

> Whenever a territorial assemblage [teacher knowledge] is taken up by a movement that deterritorializes it [accountability surveillance], we say that a machine is released ... A machine is like a set of cutting edges that insert themselves into the assemblage undergoing deterritorialization, and draw variations and mutations of it ... Effects are always machinic, in other words, [they] depend on a machine that is plugged into an assemblage and has been freed through deterritorialization ... Effects of this kind can be very diverse but are never symbolic or imaginary; they always have a real value of passage or relay. (p. 333)

Policy disqualified teacher knowledge by attacking its temporal features through the hypostatizing of performance in a test score or some other performance indicator locked in a particular time and geography. Student subjectivities were largely determined, ranked, and, in many cases, commodified a priori. Performance learning was not about learning possibilities, it was about achieving (i.e., becoming) what the accountability system had already determined were students' realistic identities and economic futures (De Lissovoy & McLaren, 2003). Indeed, teachers' professional judgments were cast as a liability, as a bias, in the new regime of truth that ultimately undermined any claims to an objective or professional territory.

The effects of deterritorializing teacher knowledge will likely produce insidious effects – effects that were not witnessed but have a reasonable chance of occurring in this contest of knowledge. For instance, the persistent absence of structures to support and protect teacher's disqualified knowledges will likely mutate professional development practices into organizational mechanisms of discipline. If this occurs, collaborative activities will be transformed into feigned symbols of teacher care that are promoted by "new school executives" (Maxcy, 1991) to subjugate teachers to new knowledges while simultaneously disqualifying endemic cognitions. Without structures to implement decisions borne of teachers' craft knowledge, "communities of practice" will become organizational mechanisms to reterritorialize teacher knowledge into assemblages that are consistent with the effective and efficient delivery of performance standards. The pressure for performativity will warp video- and audiotape professional development studies into additional ways to exterritorialize teacher knowledge. Likewise, teacher reflection will be recast as a mechanism for self-correction and auto-production rather than as a systematic study of pedagogy (Fendler, 2003). Teaching mentors within panoptic forms of accountability will be the new "[meta]technicians of behaviour" rather than guides who create knowledge with novice teachers (Foucault, 1977, p. 294). In the end, knowledge debates will be pointless because the idea of performance will have already been determined. That is, performance will have circumscribed any conceptualization of knowledge.

The microportraitures provide evidence that participants were interested in questions about teaching and learning and that some derived pleasure from engaging in these intellectual sojourns. Maya's research activities focused on the central question that participants and district personnel shared: What teaching practices improve student learning? Instead of developing cookie-cutter standards for everyone, action research provided Maya with a micromap to assist her in her nomadic journey while she engaged in fulfilling intellectual work.

The role of teacher education and professional organizations were a substantial genealogy in the development of naïve knowledges. How do teacher educators prepare teachers to mediate or resist district and state policies that do not provide sufficient latitude to meet specific student's needs? More simply, what micropolitical skills must teachers possess to use their archaic knowledges? Julie clearly would have benefited from an explicit discussion about the technical role expected of her, even if this role was antithetical to what teacher educators believed about students' professional identity.

Claire, Maya, and Julie referred to professional organizations and/or professional activities to explain the origin and development of these subjugated knowledges.[2] Only 2 participants referred to nascent beliefs – doxa – about teaching and learning. Nascent beliefs were considered to be unexamined rather than "wrong" in this research. This is an important point. Even in a district that stipulated an enormous amount of curricular and assessment policies, participants felt obligated to resist policy directives. In fact, participants' disqualified knowledges were the basis for their micropolitics. It was not possible for this knowledge to transcend or step outside the politics of their work; rather, it provided them with political hope.

For how much longer will education research continue to fuel macrowars over teachers' knowledges? How much longer will macrowars terraform teachers' cognitions? How much longer will knowledge be considered independent from power and politics? When will knowledge be recognized as a product of power and politics? When will accountability machines stop deterritorializing teachers' knowledge and, instead, tend these gardens? When will teachers act collectively?

MICROPOLITICAL GEOMETRIES

The overthrow of these "micropowers" does not, then, obey the law of all or nothing [power as a zero-sum game]; it is not acquired once and for all by a new control of the apparatuses nor by a new functioning or a destruction of the institutions; on the other hand, none of its localized episodes may be inscribed in history except by the effects that it induces on the entire network in which it is caught up.

– Foucault, *Discipline and Punish*

Teachers did not coordinate their subjugated knowledges; as a result, conflicts erupted when the school organization led participants into collective spaces (e.g., faculty meetings) that required them to discuss their work. Delphi's organization and district mandates led teachers into micropolitical encounters with each other and provided a scripted set of organizational structures that situated where these encounters took place. Teachers engaged in territorial battles over curricular policy that were coerced into being by the district. Curricular policies, then, were a formidable technology that terraformed teachers' nomadic journeys at Delphi, especially when these policies accessed the school's organization.

Figure 26 presents participants' thoughts about curriculum disagreements at Delphi. Sara's and Julie's thoughts about the reasons for the conflict over the curriculum Success for All (SFA) are of particular importance. Both participants stated that teachers shared contradictory beliefs about how to teach reading. I have

I think the faculty is split because SFA was mainly comprehension and Open Court is mainly phonics. And that's why a lot of people were split because, how do you combine those to get the best of both worlds?   – Julie

Quite a few people left. We had a fifth-grade teacher and a fourth-grade teacher that left, and both of them were against SFA. And then the principal felt like she had to leave; she got pushed out. Oh, and another teacher left because she didn't like the idea; she was the one that started the problem. But I got a hold of her information and read it, and you could tell that it was written by someone who was not really educated [about literacy]. That really angered me. – Claire

I was just at an Open Court meeting, and I could not believe the resistance from teachers. "No, I want to teach explicit phonics, and I want these children to read phonetically correct books." And I'm from the other group that would say, "That's fine, but you need to incorporate that with other things, not just with phonemics." But the phonological awareness is what they hear. I can't teach a book like that if I'm teaching a reading book in a group. It won't be phonetically correct all the time because you can't do – you cannot break down the words phonemically exactly. You're going to be using pictures for words, especially in the very beginning, when they're reading. And to me that's okay. You can't say, "You can only do it one way," because you may be getting children in other ways. I always tell parents I teach five different reading curricula in my classroom for my kids.   – Sara

Figure 26. Curricular conflicts and school politics.

represented participants' thoughts in this fashion to add importance to their testimony. The importance of Figure 26 rests not in the fact that participants disagreed about the best way to teach reading but in the nature of the disagreement. In this case, how to best teach reading was a substantive issue.

Julie's deceptively simple question – "How do you combine those [phonemic awareness and comprehension] to get the best of both worlds?" – is pregnant with additional, or latent, questions about instructional time, curricular alignment, student negotiations, and the macroreading wars. In this case, participants' nomadic journeys were circumscribed by the panoptic control of curricular policy. The effect of these emergent political spaces in Delphi redirected participants' micropolitics away from the kinds of nomadic questions raised by Julie and focused them on each other. Unfortunately, most participants did not traverse theselatent political spaces because of the coercive ways these spaces were hidden from their discussions. Participants were locked in skirmishes over the relevance of SFA rather than pursuing answers to questions such as those posed by Julie.

Past literature on school politics characterized teacher politics as disagreements about matters that relate only incidentally to the profession; for example, parking spaces, dress codes, and after-school supervision. In fact, one study characterized teachers' curricular concerns as "fears and worries" that consume the time of busy administrators whose job it is to implement state initiatives (Ball & Bowe, 1991, p. 43). Curricular debates are substantive issues, and teachers are caught in the fire zones of such wars. It should not be any surprise that teachers disagree about what is best for students when the entire enterprise of education is a political enterprise: macropolitics   micropolitics. Characterizations of teacher politics that reinforce stereotypes of teachers pose enormous barriers to moving the profession forward. Teachers may as well be asked to build skyscrapers with a pair of pliers, conduct surgery with only aspirin, or make judicial decisions from memory.

COERCIVE DETERRITORIALIZATIONS: STRATEGIC ENCOUNTERS

The process of selecting, adopting, and implementing curricular policies, when approached from the point of view of participants, turned out to be a fascinating aspect of the research. Unfortunately, evidence suggested that the district's policy adoption and implementation strategies were accompanied by coercive tactics. Natasha, the principal, provided some evidence that the district's curriculum adoption and implementation process circumvented individual schools and faculties:

> Talk about policy [implementation … I mean Quest got adopted – well it hasn't been adopted formally – but it got piloted with a huge amount of purchase last year. And, this year, they're going back and saying now we're going to go ahead and make an adoption committee after the fact. Well, the resources have been spent on a pilot, but the pilot [expenditures are] to such an extent that if the committee decides, "Well, this probably didn't work very well," the financial repercussions would be huge and probably not even

supportable to choose something else. So, it's kind of an unfortunate after-committee [thought]. I mean the committee is still going forward, and they'll make a decision, but if that kind of thing happens, our school will just have to go with it and figure out how you're going to use the materials and the curriculum.

Given that teachers used different knowledges to attend to students' welfare, I was interested in their ability to determine the educational direction of the school. I wanted to know how they responded to curricular mandates that neglected to address their own conflicted and subjugated ideas about teaching and learning. Given the range of their beliefs, I asked participants how curricular policies, particularly SFA, entered the school. Generally, participants did not understand how curricular policies were determined or how these policies entered the school. Behind this set of questions lay questions about who determined the educational direction of the school.

Success for All was a district-sponsored curriculum that required an 80% "buy-in" from the faculty. Wilson had experienced the adoption process at Delphi 4 years previously, and Natasha was teaching fifth grade when her school "adopted" SFA (different school, same district). Figures 27 and 28 provide readers with Wilson's and Natasha's thoughts about how the district coerced the initial buy-in, or consensus, for their respective schools. I have presented participants' testimony in this way so that readers can compare the similarities in participants' statements about the coercive elements at play in the district's process of adoption.

Readers should note, however, that "coercion" is the term I use to describe what participants talk about. They do not specifically use this word in their talk. However, I justify my use of the word by referring to Wilson's talk about how the district used teacher evaluation as a means to cajole acceptance. *Webster's Dictionary* (1993) stated that "coercion" means "to compel to an act or choice by force, threat, or other pressure." Wilson felt threatened that he would be unfairly assessed if he asked questions about the viability of curricula. This is a form of coercion. Also, both participants talk about the threat of transferring teachers out of their respective schools if they disagreed with SFA. This is another form of coercion.

One of the interesting aspects of Wilson's and Natasha's talk is how the district's curriculum adoption process preyed on teachers' nomadic journeys. That is, since participants had different ideas about how to teach reading, and only a short amount of time allocated to make a decision, the staff was compelled to accept SFA. Unfortunately, the district did not invest the kinds of resources to help teachers develop programs they believed would benefit their schools. Instead, the district moved the adoption process forward. Apparently it did not want to spend more money on something that was already purchased.

Teacher perception

TW: Was there ever a time when teachers were split on a curriculum issue?

Wilson: If they were split, they were gone.

TW: What?

Wilson: Yeah, [the district] transferred out, they transferred out a bunch of them. This is great, the special education teacher felt that her students weren't being served [by SFA]. She'd been teaching for a long time. She was good at what she did, but she really felt that this program ... that the kids needed it, that most weren't getting the time they needed. And she was given an administrative transfer, which is not a fire, but it doesn't look particularly good – it means you're having conflicts to the point that the principals wants you out of there. So she had to pick up all her stuff and move because she was not rolling with it, just standing up and saying, "no." She had enough sense of purpose, sense of self, to stand up and say, "No, this isn't. Bye!"

TW: How do you know this?

Wilson: When we first came up with SFA, it was really very political. I was going through a master's program at the time, and I wanted the SFA to emphasize "show me the research." And [SFA] was pretty strong in research. But I like to ask questions – that's the way I communicate, by questioning – and some of them are questions placed in the format of the devil's advocate. So, we go to these workshops, and I was marked down; they had concerns about my buy-in to the program. It was made pretty clear that if you didn't buy into the program you should transfer schools. If you were marked down as one of those people who didn't buy-in, it was reflected on my evaluation to the point where, you know, if you make waves you drown.

Figure 27. Teacher's perception of district coercion.

Principal perception

Natasha: The school I taught at also adopted SFA. It was very close in how we ended up voting for it and it was kind of like "either vote for this or you're going to lose your choice to vote" and so it was kind of like, "ok, I guess we'll do this." Because the time frame for the decision was so short there was no way we would have had time to find something else.

TW: It's kind of unfair that way.

Natasha: Yeah and with schools targeted – we had really low scores, it's like "we don't have time to fiddle around and choose something that you think you really like so here's a research based model that will work for you and if you don't like it go to another school" and I think one person left. It just wasn't comfortable for her but the rest of everyone else stuck with it and to varying degrees liked it or didn't like it. But they wanted to stay at that school so they dealt with it.

Figure 28. Principal's perceptions of district coercion.

Tactics that ignore the interests of those closest to the issues – indeed, the very people held accountable for the issues – are morally reprehensible. Repeated instances of coercion in the workplace need to be reported to local unions and governmental agencies that regulate fair and acceptable labor practices. At some point, educational improvements cannot sacrifice the integrity of those who spend their entire lives trying to do just that. It is not fair or legal. It is no wonder that Ingersoll (2003) found that the reason for the teacher shortage in the United States was their dissatisfaction with not having a formal say in curricular development in the places where they work. In this particular case, teachers were treated as obstacles rather than as solutions to complex issues of school reform and student achievement.

In an effort to respond to district coercion, the principal started to formulate the school's site council. In theory, the site council would govern the school and be responsible, in part, for its curricular, assessment, and pedagogical direction. Site councils, ironically, were an acceptable form of organizational change sanctioned by the district. However, the principal was frank about her vision for the council, given her experiences with curricular policy coercion:

> I'm just starting to work on getting a site council leadership team. And, to me, that part is to give teachers as much ownership in the decisions that we can impact, but being honest when there's a decision that we can't. Not saying, "Yes, you do get to choose whatever reading curriculum you want," and then say, "Well, actually, no you don't." I mean, if we're going to make the decision and put the time into that process, then it's because we actually have the usability to do that. If we don't, be honest and say, "You know what, these are here, this is not." But what I keep asking myself is, "How are we going to implement it in our school, keeping the focus on what's best for the kids in our school?" I mean, trying to always bring it back to the kids is hard to do sometimes because we have so many different constituencies coming at you with what they think you should do and what you think you should do. You know, it's hard.

Maya echoed Natasha's skepticism:

> You know, the district really pushed site-based management, had a lot of money available for it. But if adopting your own curriculum isn't at the crux of what site-based management is, then I don't know what is. Because *you* know what works in your building, with your kids, and your population. (My emphasis)

In theory, a site council might legitimate participants' power by producing a setting where formal decisions about curricular policies are negotiated. However, both Maya and Natasha realized that the site council might be just one more coercive form of control. Regardless of whether a site council would legitimate participants' power in a formal arena, participants clearly saw a need to move important curricular decisions away from the district and toward their school in a new organizational structure.

TANGLED SEGMENTED SPACES

We are segmented in a *binary* fashion following the great major dualist oppositions: social classes, but also men-women, adults-children, and so on. We are segmented in a *circular* fashion, in ever larger circles, ever wider disks or coronas, ... my affairs, my neighborhood's affairs, my city's, my country's, the world's ... We are segmented in a *linear* fashion, along a straight line or a number of straight lines, of which each segment represents an episode or proceduring or procedured, in the family, in the school, in the army, on the job. School tells us, "You're not at home anymore"; the army tells us, "You're not in school anymore" ... these figures of segmentarity, the binary, circular, and linear, are bound up with one another, even cross over into each other, changing according to the point of view.

– Deleuze and Guattari, *A Thousand Plateaus*

Teachers' micropolitics did not remain at the level of the classroom but seeped into the school. The significance of this finding is that the school organization is spatially constituted, producing intraschool contests over policy when teachers encountered each other as segments of their work became entangled. Delphi was segmented in at least three of the ways discussed by Deleuze and Guattari (1987):

1. In a *binary* fashion: policy-maker–teacher, teacher-student, principal-parent, and so on;
2. In a *circular* fashion: classroom, faculty meeting, school, community, and so on; and
3. In a *linear* fashion: grade levels, achievement, "meeting standard," and so on.

The school was also spatially constituted through its egg-crate architecture (see Chapter 3). I devote the next chapter to an analysis of teachers' micropolitics through a spatial lens. Many of the teachers' micropolitical encounters in the school focused on curricular policy because this deterritorializing force held the greatest threat to their antiquated knowledges. In this way, the school represented a network of power that teachers' micropolitics traversed.

District coercion signaled the primary strategy for deterritorializing teachers' knowledges. Coercion was evident when curricular policies were implemented. More importantly, policy implementation was the primary method to entangle segmented spaces, and it produced latent or invisible spaces that were hidden from teachers. Policy was able to traverse Delphi's spatialized zones, including teachers' cognitions, and reinforced the school's spatialized geometries. As a consequence, teachers' micropolitics were circumscribed: they were almost always practiced individually and often at each other, instead of being linked together to strategically address the latent spaces. Attempts to create new spaces in the school (i.e., the site council) were evidence that confirmed the spatiality of teachers' work.

And the participants' skepticism about these new spaces confirmed the coercive aspects of deterritorializing attempts. Where, then, are spaces of teachers' work not coded with district and state desires? How might teachers' nomadic journeys traverse the hidden landscapes produced from curriculum implementation? Or have teachers been effectively circumscribed from answering questions about instructional time, budgets, and so on? The tangled, segmented spaces of teachers' work contributed to their schizophrenia.

NOTES

[1] The "reading wars" are a particularly violent macrostruggle in education (Pearson, 2004). I am arguing that the violence of these macrostruggles forcibly terra-forms schools and rearranges teachers' cognitions: macropolitics   micropolitics. See Schoenfeld (2004) for a discussion of the "math wars."

[2] I believe these findings to be related to the fact that participants self-selected into the study. That is, I believe that there is some correlation between who decided to participate in the study and the kinds of professional commitments they shared. Thus, this study provided participants with ways to explore and share their practice (in addition to practices they were already engaged in).

CHAPTER 5

TEACHER ASSEMBLAGE

We evaluate to punish and almost never to improve teachers' practice. In other words, we evaluate to punish and not to educate.

− Paulo Freire, *Teachers as Cultural Workers*

The previous chapter discussed how teachers participated in the contest over their knowledge and provided detailed descriptions of the many ways teachers deliberately resisted and appropriated policy. It revealed teachers' micropolitics as a strategic way to temporarily disrupt the serious game of educator accountability. However, teachers' micropolitics were practiced in autonomous ways. These individual political acts were not coordinated and, consequently, they produced opportunities for policy to co-opt teachers' micropolitics into the accountability machine. Foucault (1982a) explained how agency can be co-opted when he noted, "People know what they do; they frequently know why they do; but what they don't know is what they do does (p. 187). Teachers' inability to know how their micropolitics affected the school created spaces in which teachers became additional agents of the accountability system − a process that Deleuze and Guattari (1987) would describe as becoming grafted or assembled onto the accountability machine. In this study, teachers were assembled onto the accountability machine when they produced pedagogical fabrications for peers to surveil. The school, then, operated within a highly complex code of micropolitical semiotics produced by teachers.

In this sense, Freire (1998) was correct: accountability policy is designed to punish teachers. However, what Freire did not explore was the process by which this disciplining occurs or the fact that teachers themselves participated in their own disciplining. Teachers' disciplining occurred when they operated as additional eyes for the accountability machine, when they mimicked or reproduced the accountability processes and intent.

This chapter examines how the game played participants.

SURVEILLANCE OF TEACHERS: UNDERSTANDING
ACCOUNTABILITY AT DELPHI

The most apparent form of surveillance at Delphi was the use of standardized tests at the school. The Washington Assessment of Student Learning (WASL) and Iowa Tests of Basic Skills (ITBS) were surveillance mechanisms that assembled data portraits of the school, which were then used to compare its performance with other schools. Test data were not used to inform instruction. For instance, when asked how test scores were used in the school, participants reported that they did not use scores to adjust instruction; rather, scores monitored teachers and the school. Wilson, the fifth-grade teacher and vice-principal, stated that test scores were used to monitor participants and the school: "District personnel use the ITBS and WASL to compare schools to each other and districts to each other, and [they] say how the school's doing as a whole and get general trends." Julie, the second-grade teacher, reported how additional measures ("benchmarks"), developed by the school district, were used to surveil teachers:

> The district requires teachers to turn all their benchmark scores in three times a year. So, the principal will collect ours, for the whole school, and then she compiles some data, tables on the computer, to show where our kids stand for each grade level on each unit. She takes that to the district and hands it in. We don't use the scores within the building. I know a lot of us feel it's kind of pointless to turn the scores in.

District and state personnel (as well as the public) were able to monitor participants' performances through reported test scores. Maya, the sixth-grade teacher, described her feelings about being surveiled by data:

> The WASL and ITBS scores are published. They're on radio; they're in the news, on the television. They are in the newspapers – I'm hypersensitive to it, being it's my job [at stake], but they're everywhere. They're on the Internet. They compare the schools to different schools.

Maya's "hypersensitivity" was the result of being compared to other schools and other teachers. Because scores were reported in aggregate, test data surveiled Maya's performance instead of providing her with diagnostic information about students' academic performance. Thus, the accountability system surveiled participants through test data and coerced them with threats of punishment, including the loss of their job (i.e., occupational death).

Surveillance Circulation: The Coercion of Unstated Expectations

Foucault (1980b) argued that surveillance and coercion circulated within organizations. He stated that "surveillance must be analysed as something which circulates, or rather as something which only functions in the form of a chain. It is never localised here or there. Power is employed and exercised through a net-like organization" (p. 98). Even though tests surveiled teachers' performances, participants also knew that the principal, other teachers, and parents observed and evaluated their practice. Judgments were made formally, through formal evaluations, and informally, through casual observations. Informal evaluations were frequent and based on public displays of teaching; for example, wall displays, public management of student behavior, and so on. Figure 29 illustrates how surveillance circulated at Delphi.

Reading facilitator
When you display children's work, teachers constantly monitor what everyone puts on the walls, and it sort of makes you as a teacher go, "Wow, she or he did that in their room, that is pretty cool." Or, if you've put a sloppy display up, I think that reflects on you as well. I know the reading facilitator has made a lot of judgments [about the quality of teaching] based upon what she has seen in the hallways.

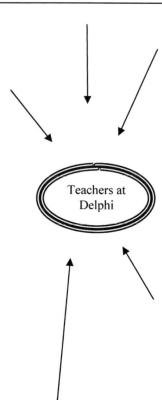

Parents
The parent that I found spent the most time in my classroom was from a Russian child who was going to be here too short a time to be taught in an English as a Second Language classroom. They were full. So she knew a little bit of English, and I was asked if I would take her on for the 2 months or so that she was here. Her mother was there for like a day and a half trying to figure out how things worked before she was pretty sure that nothing bad was going to happen.

Curriculum developers
Curriculum developers (SFA) frequently evaluated us. It was very threatening because they had a big checklist. They were checking off everything we were doing for 2 or 3 minutes. They were checking on us often, keeping us on track because they have a vested interest in our performances.

Teachers at Delphi

Principal
The principal comes in and out every once in awhile just to see how things are going. She'll just come in and out without us knowing ahead of time.

Other teachers
When I see somebody walking kids in the hallway quietly, I don't necessarily think, "That's a good teacher." However, people believe that teachers who have trouble with their kids in the hallways are the ones whose kids are always in the office – when you pass their classroom all you hear is chaos – who have trouble managing their classroom. The logic is, they can't teach because they can't manage their classroom. So that's a quick and dirty strategy [to uphold the appearance of good teaching]. And no one has to go into classrooms to see, you know.

Figure 29. Capillary nodes of surveillance.

The figure suggests a "fishbowl," with teachers being the objects of attention from several different vantage points.

Macropolitical ↔ Micropolitical

Readers should not overlook the relationship between the macrodesire to surveil teachers and micro-instances of those desires. Figure 29 not only represents the panoptic power circulating within Delphi but also how community members internalized and mimicked those desires. Thus, Figure 29 represents how power circulated within the institution and flowed between the external policy networks.

Foucault (1980b) believed that the "capillary" aspect of power had methodological implications for those who studied it (p. 39):

> Power must by [*sic*] analysed as something which circulates, or rather as something which only functions in the form of a chain. It is never localised here or there, never in anybody's hands, never appropriated as a commodity or piece of wealth. Power is employed and exercised through a net-like organisation. (p. 98)

The idea that power is exercised rather than possessed disqualifies notions that only people in positions of authority in hierarchical organizations use power. Everyone uses power, and everyone is subjected to it. Contemporary organizational theorists have noted that modern organizations (schools) have moved away from structures built on hierarchies of authority (Bolman & Deal, 1991). These "flattened" organizations delegate responsibilities to a larger number of members, thereby decreasing the layers of management (Witherspoon, 1997). This is particularly true in attempts to decentralize schools from existing bureaucratic controls. However, at Delphi the flattened organizational structure only dispersed and intensified the gaze while simultaneously obfuscating the district's and state's role in exercising surveillance. From this vantage point, the state was able to steer Delphi from a distance by fostering the illusion that participants were in control of the school's direction (Marceau, 1993). Power to define the ways policy operated was more important than the power to define policy outcomes.

Fraser (1989) distinguished surveillance mechanisms from the expectations they enforce. For instance, surveillance cameras on metro busses enforce the expectation that passengers pay their fare. Fraser (1989, p. 29) argued that an analysis that only identified surveillance mechanisms would not be "capable of specifying who is dominating whom and who is resisting whom." Fraser pointed out that the way expectations are used in surveillance schemes determines the effectiveness of the attempt to influence. For instance, returning to Figure 29, Maya noted that the school's reading facilitator informally evaluated her practice based on the bulletin boards she displayed outside her classroom. However, the reading facilitator did not disclose the criterion on which she made her evaluation. Consequently, Maya believed that her bulletin boards conformed to the reading facilitator's expectations because she received a good report.

A closer examination of Figure 29 illustrates the coercive aspects of surveillance in its capillary form. Data in Figure 29 describes attempts to coerce participants by circulating unstated expectations (as opposed to absent expectations). For instance, what is the principal looking for when she appears unannounced in Julie's classroom? When I asked Natasha why she appeared in Julie's classroom announced, Natasha mentioned that she wanted to check on the relatively new teacher to "make sure everything was okay." However, the rationale of inexperience did not fully explain the reasons for announced visits, as several other senior participants also commented on Natasha's surprise visits. Vague expectations regarding unexpected principal visits were a prevalent form of power circulation at Delphi, and they provide another example of how people become the vehicles of power and regulation.

Another example of how unstated expectations coerced participants is illustrated in the talk of Claire. As is indicated in Figure 29, Claire discussed how surveillance regulated the foot traffic at Delphi. Claire explained that she felt coerced to walk students quietly based on the normative logic that quiet students equaled pedagogical competence. Sara, the kindergarten teacher, confirmed that surveillance was used to regulate her practice in the hallways:

Teachers watch [other] teachers walk in the hallways to make judgments about them. As a new teacher, I was concerned about what other teachers would think of me by how my kids walked in the hallway. I'm not as concerned about that anymore [6 years later]. My big push now is that they need to walk quietly in the hallway because they are going to disturb other classes, not so much what other teachers think about [my teaching].

Lukes (1974) argued that mechanisms in the "third face" of power are used to shape people's interests. Data from this study support this claim. Surveillance was the mechanism that shaped participants' preferences for walking quietly down the hall. For instance, Sara's testimony provided evidence that she developed new preferences for existing practices because she was surveiled. Claire's testimony also confirmed Lukes' claim (see Figure 29). Participants developed preferences for walking quietly because of the unstated expectations that circulated about this practice. This form of coercion is somewhat different from Warren's (1968) speculation that coercion was a product of threatened (or actual) punishment. While participants feared reprimands and possible censure, they developed preferences for practices because of the intense pressure of being watched discreetly. Sara's acquired preference for walking students quietly resulted from concerns about "being different" rather than from fear of punishment.

Power Circulation as Efficient Regulation

The capillary nature of power is one constitutive condition. As noted, panoptic technologies are also efficient: they do not even have to work to achieve intended results. The exercise of power is made possible with few human resources, which reduces costs. Wirt and Kirst (1997) argued that efficiency might be the most sought out value in educational policy because of the limited amount of resources in the system. They stated that policy acts as a form of accountability that serves "the end of responsibility for the exercise of public authority and the local exercise of power" (p. 70). Accountability policies, then, are efficient panoptic mechanisms when they are conceived as a galvanizing symbol; for instance, a policy that carries no decrees but governs the meaning of an organization. Malen and Knapp (1997) argued that "policy is constructed to shape public meanings and produces effects largely through its impact on audiences' perceptions of problems, priorities, and possibilities" (p. 431). Policy itself can be a panoptic technology because people control their behavior to conform to their own interpretation of policy. Obvious examples of both the panoptic and dialectical conditions are the policy and schooling dynamics that play out in high-stakes assessment and accountability environments.

Surveillance circulation at Delphi prompted teachers to develop their own sense of accountability, as was suggested by Abelmann and Elmore (1999). Even though it was largely unstated and highly coercive, the accountability system at Delphi regulated teachers' practices by circulating unstated expectations, which were monitored by surveillance. For instance, Wilson noted that

> observations *are not even actually physically there* most of the time. It's "What are you sending home for homework? How well can they do the homework, you know? What are my expectations of your child? Do they get slapped with bad news without any preparation about their kid?" That's the kind of observation I'm talking about. Not the kinds where people come into your classroom to check things out. (My emphasis)

The capillary effects of surveillance caused participants to internalize definitions of accountability at Delphi. We could describe the kind of educator accountability that prevailed at Delphi as a system of *paranoid* or *suspicious* accountability. This paranoiac system was so powerful that participants regulated their practice even when surveillance mechanisms were not present, as is evident in Wilson's discussion of "anonymous" observations. Claire, as is shown in Figure 29, confirmed the capillary and anonymous power of the paranoiac system to regulate teachers when she stated, "No one has to go into classrooms to see [teachers], you know." Claire regulated her practice even in the absence of direct monitoring. The net effect of the paranoiac system is that teachers controlled themselves through a complex system of unspoken and/or unstated expectations.

Surveillance Reproduction at Delphi: The Paranoiac Form of Self-Governance

Foucault (1980b) theorized that the capillary effects of surveillance were an efficient way to regulate employees. However, the most efficient method to regulate teachers is to generate conditions in which they surveil themselves. Like a copy<This simile is unclear>, participants monitored their peers and themselves, reproducing the effects of surveillance in the school. This was evident in the ways teachers monitored their peers in the hallways.

The final constitutive condition of power is the synthesis of the two prior conditions (efficient and capillary) with power's ability to reproduce itself. Power aims to "increase both the docility and the utility of all the elements of the system" (Foucault, 1984a, p. 207). Foucault believed that panoptic technologies sought out more and more ways to maximize both their coverage and their economy because of the persistent need to regulate and control a growing population. Power reproduces itself when it is able to monitor more while keeping the costs of doing so low. (See Foucault's [1977, 1984b] discussion of the three constitutive elements of modern power in his chapter titled "Panopticism."). Clegg (1989) provided a definition of surveillance reproduction:

Power ... is regularized, routinized, cast as a constant surveillance constituting a new discipline of norms and behaviour. [Employees] of whatever institution would be acutely aware that their every action might be ... subject to the supervisory gaze of surveillance. This knowledge in itself might be sufficient to produce disciplined obedience, as subjects learned literally to survey themselves, to be reflexively self-regarding as if under the ever-present and watchful eye of surveillance. (pp. 173-174)

Why did participants monitor themselves and their peers, given the stiflingly amount of surveillance already in place? Maya, the sixth-grade teacher, provided an answer to that question:

Teachers are making [informal] observations of you based on maybe one thing. And if they saw a lesson that went great or they happen to see a project that you did, the impression of that project or lesson carries over. And so everything you do from that point on already starts a level up because they are looking at you with a different lens.

A major theme in Maya's talk is the idea that surveillance identifies "good" teachers. Conversely, participants also believed they could identify "bad" teachers through surveillance. Julie stated:

You start to get the feeling when a teacher's slacking or when it really is a bad teacher. And you're aware of it, and you know when a teacher is not teaching as academically, as enhancing as it could be. You start to pick up on that. They're pulling the VCR more than they should be, and they're spending a lot of time just in front of the copying machine, just copying everything off. So there's an awareness that goes on. You almost never have the opportunity to formally observe another teacher at work. Very seldom, which is a shame because you can learn a lot. By not talking to each other, you miss out on a lot of that stuff. Teachers put so much time into developing ideas, you lose it or you don't get to utilize it when we don't talk to each other.

Attempts to evaluate peers informally prompted participants to reproduce surveillance. In fact, Julie suggested that discreet observations of teachers could substitute for absent organizational structures that could help teachers learn about their work. Instead of developing formal structures to learn about their work, participants evaluated their peers informally – around the copy machine, in the hallways, at staff meetings, and so on. Other than normative and unstated expectations (doxa), participants had little criteria to help them determine teaching quality at Delphi and no formal structures to do so. Without explicit organizational structures to facilitate teacher learning, participants reproduced governments' and the public's suspicion of their abilities when they internalized the accountability gaze and tried to determine who was "slacking."

CHOREOGRAPHY OF ACCOUNTABILITY

There are indications here of the particular performativity – the management of performance – which is "called up" by inspection. What is produced is a spectacle, or game-playing, or cynical compliance, or what one might see as an "enacted fantasy,' which is there simply to be seen and judged – a fabrication.

– Stephen Ball, "The Teacher's Soul and the
Terrors of Performativity"

Teachers created fabrications to respond to the flow of surveillance that was used to control them. Participants knew that pedagogical performances represented their professional status and therefore could be used as political capital to shape evaluations of their practice. They mutated pedagogy into objects for viewing and circulated images of these objects in a micropolitical spectacle. Wilson noted the use of fabrication in his teaching:

If I don't believe in what I'm teaching, then I will subvert it. I will change it. When the doors are open, they will see something different than when the doors are closed. So, if I don't believe in what I'm teaching, or what I'm told to teach, then I won't do it. I'm putting on – I'm doing two sets of lesson plans. Kind of like keeping two sets of books – you have the set of books for the auditors and you have the set of books that you're really doing your stuff.

Wilson's fabrications were responses to curricular demands that ostracized his professional discretion. His fabrications literally hinged on providing surveilers visible access to his classroom practice. Wilson's analogy to the corporate practice of cooked books indicates that he is also aware of accountability performances in the business world.

As noted above, unannounced visits by the school principal were a persistent form of surveillance used to coerce teachers, and a specific fabrication – student performance assessments, or portfolios – were used to control the principal's impressions. Wilson described how he fabricated portfolios to manage his principal's impressions of him as a teacher:

I keep portfolios of the kids' work, and I assess quite frequently, and so the principal assumes that I'm a good teacher. She's popped into my classroom [unannounced] and asked me, "How are you going to teach this and this?" and "How are you going to assess it?" Kind of this bullshit thing we do. And you know, I'm prepared now. I show her the portfolios. Mind you, I don't have to show *what's in* the portfolio – just the idea that I have a portfolio [indicates to her that] I'm on the ball. I don't take out the [evidence] to show, for instance, "here are the writing pieces, and here's evidence for reading and math." No, just the idea that I've got the portfolio and it looks official – it's got the kid's name on it, it's got my name on, and it's got the principal's name on it. She assumes that I'm on top of things. She said to me one time, "Well good, I don't have to worry about you."

Portfolios were representations of performativity in addition to classroom heuristics to explain student performance. While observations confirmed that Wilson assessed students with portfolios, portfolios were also organizational fabrications that controlled impressions through a choreographed script of self-promotion and/or pedagogical exemplification. Pedagogic simulations, therefore, played a dual role in Wilson's work: they were products of classroom activity and representations of pedagogy used within the school to shape impressions. Ball (2003) discussed the dual nature of fabrications:

Fabrications are not "outside the truth" but neither do they render simply true or direct accounts – they are produced purposefully in order "to be accountable." Truthfulness is not the point – the point is their effectiveness, for Inspection or appraisal, and in the "work" they do "on" and "in" the organization. (p. 224)

To shape surveilers' reality, teachers created additional fabrications, including the use of bulletin boards, or public displays of classroom activity, which were often placed in hallways adjacent to teachers' classrooms. One teacher noted:

I know the reading facilitator has made a lot of judgments [about the quality of teaching] based upon what she has seen in the hallways. And so everything you do from that point on already starts a level up because they are looking at you with a different lens. The facilitator will make judgments of you based on that one observation, and, if they liked what they saw, the impression carries over. I am very careful about what goes up on the bulletin boards.

Like portfolios, bulletin boards were pedagogic simulations – signs of teaching prowess circulated to manage impressions.

Beneath participants' use of fabrication lay professional knowledge that recognized how to present oneself within particular registers of meaning. However, because of the uncertainty of being evaluated differently by different agents, fabrications held approximate political capital for those who used them.

Micropolitical Semiotics: Approximate Micropolitical Strategies

Fabrications were effective micropolitical resources when they aligned with surveilers' expectations; that is, "successful" fabrications communicated credible and competent professional status in ways that fulfilled surveilers' expectations. Wilson's use of portfolios is one example. However, attempts at impression management carried the risk of being perceived negatively. For every desired image sought by teachers, an undesired image was risked. For instance, Wilson described situations where portfolios were not successful fabrications:

> Portfolios have not been a way to develop my reputation among other teachers because nobody knows about them. We don't have those conversations – "Who's using portfolios? Let's see what portfolios look like." I mean several teachers just don't know about portfolios.

The uncertainty of being judged in different ways, by different agents, limited teachers' abilities to use fabrications consistently. As a result, fabrications were political approximations intended to present oneself within shifting registers of meaning – a process others described as "self-monitoring" when used to manage impressions (Turnley & Bolino, 2001). In this study, participants calculated fabrications from "pedagogic-simulation reasoning" – a form of thought that estimated risks associated with presenting oneself in multiple and fluctuating registers of meaning. When creating fabrications, participants considered (1) who was watching their work, (2) the expectations these people might have, (3) possible pedagogies to fabricate, (4) strategies to maximize desired images, and (5) strategies to minimize unintended or undesired images. Walking students through school hallways – quietly and in single file – was an example of a "risky" fabrication. Claire remarked:

> The most obvious status builder at our school is walking in the hallways. More importantly, "Do you have control of your children?" If you have control of your children, then you're a good teacher. Forget about your knowledge base. I mean that's really a quick and dirty strategy that the principal and other teachers use to [evaluate] teachers. When I see somebody walking his or her kids in the hallway quietly, I don't necessarily think, "That's a good teacher." People believe [however] that teachers who have trouble with their kids in the hallways are the ones who have trouble managing their classroom. The logic is they can't teach because they can't manage the kids. So that's a quick and dirty strategy [to uphold the appearance of good teaching]. And no one has to go into classrooms to see, you know.

The risks associated with fabricating students' behavior in the hallways were appearing "obviously fabricated" or "clearly inauthentic." Another teacher explained that those who appeared obviously fabricated did so at the risk of student learning:

Teachers use "walking in the hallways" to make judgments about other teachers. As a new teacher, I was much more concerned about it than I am now because I was concerned about what other teachers would think of me by how my kids walked in the hallway. I'm not nearly as concerned about that anymore, although I believe they need to walk quietly in the hallway because they are going to disturb other classes – not so much what other teachers think [about my teaching]. I wouldn't argue that walking in a straight line is quality teaching. It's just a kind of teaching. It's a kind of quiet teaching. Just because there is noise going on in a classroom doesn't mean its chaos. In fact, attempts to be strict lose a lot of kids in the classroom.

These data illustrated what participants thought about the possibilities of inauthentic performances – performances that might sacrifice student learning for the sake of promoting professional reputations. The fabrication played an important role in the school as a sign of pedagogic excellence for those who used the fabrication as a micropolitical resource. However, because fabrications risked subjecting students to inauthentic learning experiences, teachers attempted to appear genuine, or, in other words, teachers wrestled with what was or was not educationally "authentic."

Micropolitical Semiotics: Crises of Authenticity

Participants were concerned about subjecting students to inauthentic performances. This study identified these concerns as "crises of authenticity," which were evident when teachers wrestled with their own professional judgments, students' needs, and the demands for performativity. Jeffrey (2002) identified similar psychic conditions and described teachers as possessing "multiple selves" and "restructured identities," while Ball (2003) noted that crises of performativity act as a kind of "values schizophrenia" for teachers.

Wilson described his feelings about subjecting students to inauthentic performances:

The more they [district administrators] emphasize something that I don't believe in, the more I become paralyzed and ineffectual. I'm teaching something I don't agree with. I'm being forced to teach in a certain way [a fabrication]. I try to do the other one [authentic teaching] in a way that's not drawing the attention of the administrators too much, but it becomes paralyzing. You find yourself wallowing instead of teaching. And, so, the kids become the real losers, with teachers who don't believe in what they're doing [don't believe in the fabrication].

McNeil (2000) described teachers' demoralization when "teaching to the test" – the internal doubts that are produced when states emphasize high scores instead of student learning. In this study, the phrase "teaching for the test" is a better description of the performativity pressure felt by participants. As noted in the previous chapter, the pressure to perform was so great that participants said that their teaching was becoming more and more fabricated. The pressure to perform was also creating new identities, as Maya noted with reference to her own experience: "I am becoming more and more teacher-directed every day, and this is not what teaching should be." Finally, once performance expectations trumped issues that had an impact on the participants' ability to do the work, participants questioned their commitment to the job:

> My personal goal of trying to help all kids become excited lifelong learners can't be fulfilled for many different reasons – large class size, lack of an inviting, pleasant, high-quality facility for kids, lack of up-to-date textbooks, and enough of them for all students. Some students are in emotionally dysfunctional homes. There are days that you go home and you think, "Why am I doing this? Should I be doing this?" It's becoming something of a drain.

MICROPOLITICAL SEMIOTICS: CO-OPTED ORGANIZATIONAL RESOURCES

Because fabrications were approximate calculations, participants equivocated (hedged) between a fabrication's political potential and its expected pedagogical value. In other words, there were times when participants would downplay a fabrication's pedagogical value in favour of emphasizing its political value within the school. In these instances, participants simply acquired preferences that sustained fabrications because of the "correct" meaning they denoted in the schools. Ball (2001) observed how performativity co-opts the organization when teachers transform their practice into the accumulation of fabrications:

> Organizational fabrications are an escape from the gaze, a strategy of impression management that in effect erects a façade of calculation. But in another sense the work of fabricating the organisation requires submission to the rigours of performativity and the disciplines of competition – resistance and capitulation. It is, as few have seen, a betrayal even, a giving up of claims to authenticity and commitment, it is an investment in plasticity. Crucially and invariably acts of fabrication and the fabrications themselves act and reflect back upon the practices they stand for. The fabrication becomes something to be sustained, lived up to. Something to measure individual practices against. The discipline of the market is transformed into the discipline of the image, the sign. (p. 217)

Surveillance coerced participants to use fabrications as specific signs within the school – the most notable examples being test scores and the management of student behavior in hallways. Bulletin boards and portfolios were approximate signs that contained greater risks because expectations for these particular fabrications varied greatly. While participants feared rebuke for producing "poor performances," they perpetuated some fabrications because they worried more about being different than they feared punishment. This form of coercion differed somewhat from Warren's (1968) speculation that coercion was a product of threatened (or actual) punishment. Instead, participants' beliefs were shaped from a kind of "dominant ideology," as expressed by Lukes (1974). That is, the omnipresent and ever watchful eye of surveillance coerced participants to walk students quietly and in single file – the dominant practice of the schools. Participants knew they were expected to walk students quietly, they knew that they were being watched, but their reasons for doing so were mutable or plastic.

The school co-opted teachers' fabrications to increase accountability production. The most significant evidence supporting this claim was the fact that teachers maintained fabrications for their peers to surveil. Surveillance created conditions wherein participants became additional agents of the external accountability system, not self-governing agents of their own expectations. Participants coerced peers by surveiling practice to enforce school norms. As noted, teachers surveiled peers in hallways, in lunchrooms, during assemblies, on the playground, and with regard to their bulletin boards. Thus, participants reproduced the coercion of the external accountability system by discreetly watching their peers inside the school. Participants cultivated an "awareness" of their peers' abilities by surveiling their performances, which led to the institutionalization of specific fabrications. Instead of resisting surveillance practices and inauthentic fabrications, participants appropriated them and amplified their effect within the schools.

Fabrications were created to be seen and judged; they were Baudrillardian signs designed to be consumed within the microspectacle of the school. Fabrications were circulated to control surveilers' impressions; they were adept micropolitical resources to control the meaning of participants' professional status. Thus, in addition to the ubiquitous closing of the classroom door, participants developed additional strategies to protect themselves. Fabrications were part of a hierarchical system of meaning within the schools. Portfolios, for instance, were excellent fabrications to persuade principals, but they failed to persuade some colleagues. Conversely, participants who chose not to use expected fabrications, or who were unaware that pedagogy was emblematic, risked punishment: poor test scores (censure), not walking students in single file (ostracism), putting up a bad bulletin board (poor evaluation). Participants used fabrications as currency within the school, as signs of prestige and status exchanged for (micro)political capital. Simulations raised important questions of pedagogical authenticity that blurred the line of what is and is not "real." Put another way, participants' simulations raised questions about whose expectations were being fulfilled – those of teachers, policy-makers, or others? Who controlled classroom pedagogy? Who controlled school culture? Who controlled student learning?

Although participants were powerful within the schools, participants' power, and ultimately their professional agency, was seriously circumscribed. The most obvious limitation on the participants' power was the existence of external expectations – for test scores, student behavior, and curricular prowess (e.g., portfolios). Because fabrications blurred the boundary between the real and the unreal, school and classroom expectations were camouflaged, reproduced, and simulated. This is dangerous. Those with explicit knowledge of surveillance and coercion could use such monitoring practices in stealth to institute particular organizational preferences. Because coercion and surveillance were used anonymously, it is not clear whose professional goals were sustained. Consequently, pedagogic simulations maintained the school's cultural norms and masked the processes that defined these norms. This was evident when participants developed preferences for practices they disliked.

Simulating pedagogy left teachers fabricated and assembled. Foucault (1977) noted the implications of such a statement:

> The individual is no doubt the fictitious atom of an "ideological" representation of society; but he [sic] is also a reality fabricated by this specific technology of power that I have called "discipline." We must cease once and for all to describe the effects of power in negative terms: it "excludes," it "represses," it "censors," it "abstracts," it "masks," it "conceals." In fact, power produces; it produces reality; it produces domains of objects and rituals of truth. (p. 194)

Insidiously, surveillance was a form of accountability that coerced teachers to advocate for and implement fabrications that were not to their benefit. Participants were co-opted into accountability production. When participants generated fabrications, they amplified the external accountability production. Foucault (1977) explained how surveillance reproduced:

> Hence the major effect of [surveillance is] to induce in the [employee] a state of conscious and permanent visibility that assures the automatic functioning of power. So to arrange things that the surveillance is permanent in its effects, even if it is discontinuous in its action, which the employee should be caught up in a power situation of which they are themselves the bearers. (p. 201)

The steady flow of surveillance, peer and otherwise, was so pervasive that participants noted how it regulated their practice, even when surveillance mechanisms were not physically present. The threat of being watched was sufficient to fabricate practice in ways that were institutionally "correct." For example, a re-examination of Wilson's impressions of surveillance indicates the coercion produced from "anonymous" surveillance: "Observations are not even actually physically there most of the time." Another compelling piece of evidence about the ways participants regulated themselves was Claire's awareness of being surveiled in the hallways. She noted, "No one has to go into classrooms to see, you know." Participants knew that their work was being surveiled constantly and anonymously, and they regulated themselves accordingly.

Cognitive Colonization ↔ Teacher Assemblage

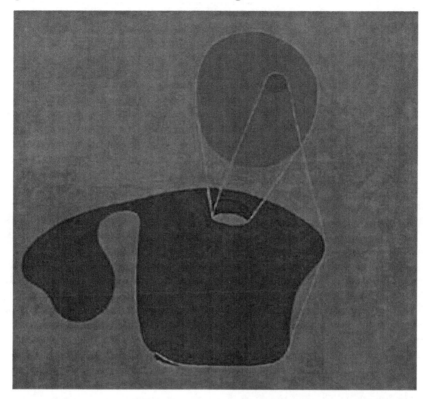

Figure 30. Meret Oppenheim. Red head, blue body. 1936. © Estate of Meret Oppenheim / SODRAC (2008)

Teachers calculated fabrications from pedagogical simulation reasoning – a strategic form of teacher cognition that estimates the risks associated with presenting oneself in multiple and competing registers of meaning. Meret Oppenheim's (1936) "Red head, blue body" depicts a kind of assemblage remenassant of a puppet. In Oppenheim's painting, the cognitive is tied, or assembled, to the body. Thus, pedagogical simulation reasoning is cognitive resistance and capitulation, suicide and rebirth (Loeb, 2007). Pedagogical simulation reasoning, consequently, was a form of strategic cognition that attempted to reterritorialize teacher knowledge. In fact, a codified "knowledge base" of pedagogy was needed only as a base for fabrications within systems of accountability surveillance: knowledge of cognitive strategies to refract, resist, criticize, and reterritorialize accountability surveillance are now the necessary tactics needed from educator preparation programs. While pedagogical simulation reasoning was an endemic form of political resistance – or a situated form of teachers' *political knowledge* – it raises important questions of pedagogical authenticity and judgment. What was or was not real or authentic? Are the expectations of teachers, policy-makers, or others fulfilled when teachers reterritorialize? How were fabricated epistemologies learned and maintained?

States and local school districts need to support teacher discretion instead of devising more ways to eliminate it through accountability threats. Governmental bodies that continue to neglect the idea of quality professional development run a serious risk of liability when they breach the public trust about schooling. States and school districts breach a moral imperative when they infer that the problems of education fall squarely on "non-compliant" teachers. This breach is exacerbated when teachers are excluded from developing initiatives aimed to improve the conditions for schooling at their local sites, sites where teachers may in fact know more about students' needs than policy-makers. Policy practices that elide the interests of those closest to the issues, indeed, the very people held accountable for the issues, are morally dubious. It is time for school districts and governments to become accountable to teachers (Sirotnik, 2004). School districts and governments are also accountable to the reform literature that exists and should quickly facilitate opportunities for teacher learning.

Teacher education must also help teachers develop a coherent professional identity in addition to helping them to become competent in subject matter pedagogy. By doing so, teacher education – education that directly and explicitly discusses teachers' discretion, responsibilities, and rights – will have much more impact on the inevitable exercise of power in schools. This education should be directed toward the responsible exercise of autonomy. Teachers also need to recommit to their profession and assume more visible roles that demonstrate their skills, knowledge, and expertise. If this occurs, teachers – not policy-makers – would make visible what everyone is searching for.

Finally, these schools need structures that support a deliberative work environment. Participants would have benefited from structured time so they could discuss issues related to teaching, student learning, leadership, and decision making. Moreover, these structures must support teachers in the collaborative practices that inform the work of teaching and learning. The work of the school concerns teaching and learning, and leaders must develop practices, procedures, and resources for that work to be supported and developed systematically.

MIMICRY, REPRODUCTION, AND LIBIDINAL PRODUCTION: POLICY IMPLICATIONS

Using data from a case study, this analysis continues the theoretical development of surveillance as a form of educational accountability. Specifically, the study illustrates how teachers thought about and enacted school accountability practices. However, rather than exhibiting a straightforward response to high stakes, teachers cultivated a form of accountability that relied on elements of visibility and coercion in the external surveillance system. Therefore, teachers' responses to the accountability system must be understood as a *form* and *function* of accountability rather than as a simple policy result. The significance of this relationship was illustrated by the extent to which the accountability process, not simply the accountability intent, influenced teachers. The analysis indicated that the implementation and enactment of accountability had as much, and potentially more, influence on educator practice than did the consequences of failing to comply with external directives. In fact, teachers were held accountable to the cultural norms of the school in ways that duplicated the visible intent of the external surveillance system. Understanding the relationship between the form and function of accountability deepens knowledge of accountability policy by identifying social values, policy decisions, and organizational norms that prompt and enforce educator regulation.

Understanding the Form and Function of Accountability: An Efficient System

My discussion of the form and function of Delphi's accountability system is informed by the theoretical framework that guided my interpretation of the case. Because a single case study cannot generalize findings to populations or settings, I limit my discussion to those generalizations that can me made. I develop "analytical generalizations" (Yin, 1989), or statements that pertain to the theory that guided the investigation, which Becker (1990) referred to as "generalizations to theory." I conclude with suggestions about the ways accountability is conducted in relation to accountability expectations.

To understand the form of accountability at Delphi, it is necessary to understand the choices teachers and policy-makers made to implement the accountability system. To understand the function of accountability at Delphi, it is necessary to understand teacher expectations; more precisely, it is necessary to understand how teacher expectations were enforced.

Policy-makers selected tests as visibility mechanisms rather than selecting visibility mechanisms (e.g., networks, study groups, or teacher inquiry) to improve teacher learning. However, test data were not used to inform participants of their students' performances because results were never reported to teachers (and teachers did not score these assessments). Instead, scores were published through the media as ways to coerce teachers. In fact, policy-makers missed or ignored opportunities to support participants' requests for local forms of accountability that would increase their learning and knowledge.

Teachers did, however, mediate accountability mechanisms, but not necessarily in ways suggested by the literature. Instead of ignoring accountability mandates, participants were very anxious about their potential effects. Instead of simply resisting accountability mechanisms, participants appropriated them. Thus, teachers amplified surveillance or, in Foucauldian terms, reproduced surveillance and used it to regulate their peers and themselves in their own paranoiac enactment of school accountability.

There are two important analytic statements that support such an assertion. First, participants utilized a system of opaque expectations to coerce peers and enforce school norms. Thus, participants *reproduced the form* of surveillance by discreetly watching their peers inside the school, and they *reproduced the function* of surveillance by coercing peers through unstated expectations for their work. Surveillance and coercion were such an efficient accountability dynamic that participants acquired preferences for teaching practices they disliked and maintained these preferences in the absence of direct monitoring. Unfortunately, teachers were not aware of the extent to which their professional discretion was being eroded by their participation in this paranoiac form of accountability. And their complicity masked opportunities to participate in overt goal setting.

The second analytic statement refers to participants' professional identity in relation to the *equivocation of accountability function* and the *equivocation of accountability form*. Because participants regulated themselves, surveillance was a highly efficient way to control teachers. In fact, participants self-regulated. Therefore, a (specious) argument could be made that surveillance was a highly efficient mechanism to produce self-governance. However, such an argument would be unsustainable because participants did not develop accountability expectations that would benefit their students and themselves. State standards did not provide participants with sufficient guidance to manage student learning in relation to poverty, multilinguistic and/or multicultural populations, and for families who had high mobility rates in the community. Increased accountability pressure, in light of generic expectations, created conditions in which participants became additional agents of the external accountability system, not self-governing agents of their own expectations. Participants possessed an illusory sense of professional power that would register incorrectly on quantitative studies (e.g., surveys) that measured self-efficacy or some other variable related to self-perceptions of professional power.

Thus, teachers maintained the status quo of the school. Insidiously, surveillance was a form of accountability that coerced teachers to advocate for, and implement, preferences from which they derived no benefit. Participants' accountability decisions were dichotomous, and the school's accountability intent fragmented. Even though participants shared access to power, they decided to surveil themselves and their colleagues instead of working together to develop criteria for "good" teaching and ways to demonstrate it. Participants' dichotomous decisions resulted from the unequal effects of power and prevented them from developing requests that would support their needs. The overwhelming amount of surveillance, designed to identify "bad" teachers, preempted definitions of "good" teaching and prohibited opportunities for participants to develop professional obligations on their terms (and in relation to state standards, for example). Power circulation and reproduction provided both individual autonomy and collective disintegration. Participants could almost observe what they wanted in the school, but they decided not to interact substantively and intellectually with their colleagues.

Surveillance, then, presents serious problems when used in accountability schemes. Even though participants self-regulated their practice, this form of autonomous control was a highly suspect form of professional maintenance. For instance, would other schools adopt such a paranoiac model of accountability and professional governance? It is quite clear that those teachers with explicit knowledge of surveillance and coercion could intentionally use monitoring practices to institute particular organizational preferences in stealth. Because coercion and surveillance circulated anonymously, it is not clear whose professional goals were being sustained. As a consequence, the efficiency with which surveillance operated at Delphi maintained the school's cultural norms and masked the processes that defined these norms. This was evident when participants developed preferences for practices they disliked.

Given the importance of accountability's form and function, as discussed here, paying attention to how accountability is conducted is as important as developing sound and explicit accountability expectations. A growing literature, both old and new, insists that states, school districts, and schools play an important role in developing conditions for teacher learning rather than teacher obedience (Goodlad 1975, Borko, 2004). Districts, governments, and media that continue to neglect this idea run a serious risk of liability when they infer that the problems of education fall squarely on "non-compliant" or "lazy" teachers.

Additionally, states and districts breach a moral imperative when they break the public trust about schooling. This breach is exacerbated when teachers are excluded from developing initiatives to improve the conditions for schooling at their local sites, sites where some teachers may know more about students' needs than policy-makers (Elmore, 2005; Hargreaves, 1996). Policy practices that ignore the interests of those closest to the issues – indeed, the very people held accountable for the issues – are morally dubious. It is time that school districts and governments become accountable to the high-quality reform literature that exists and begin to facilitate opportunities for teacher learning. Evidence from this discussion suggests that teachers at Delphi not only wished for learning opportunities, they would likely reproduce these practices quite well.

Teachers, therefore, should stop negotiating with these machines and take matters into their own hands by transforming themselves deliberately and consciously. Foucault (1984a) noted the microchoices people make with regard to producing themselves. With the help of a notorious surrealist, Foucault (1984a) stated:

> Modern man [sic], for Baudelaire, is not the man who goes off to discover himself, his secrets and his hidden truth; he is the man who tries to invent himself. This modernity does not "liberate man in his own being"; it compels him to face the task of producing himself." (p. 42)

It remains to be seen, however, if teachers prefer their disciplining, external transmogrification, and schizophrenia to the option of direct intervention and self-care.

THE (MICRO)POLITICS OF SUBJECTIVITY

How Might Teachers Be?

Once there exists, in a culture, a true discourse on the subject, what experience does the subject have of his [or her] self?

> – Foucault, *Subjectivité et vérité* (quoted and translated in Parras, 2006, p. 124)

This is how it should be done: Lodge yourself on a stratum, experiment with the opportunities it offers, find an advantageous place on it, find potential movements of deterritorialization, possible lines of flight, experience them, produce flow conjunctions here and there, try out continuums of intensities segment by segment, have a small plot of new land at all times.

> – Deleuze and Guattari, *A Thousand Plateaus*

There is no shortage of literature that purports to describe what teachers should be. That is, enormous literatures exist that describe teaching subjectivities, how teachers ought to be helped, encouraged, supported, prepared, educated, compensated, included, facilitated, and so on. Of course, these claims about teachers' subjectivities are often conflated with explicit political claims. In the political spaces governing teachers' bodies, teachers should be more proficient, effective, involved, caring, fair, efficient, knowledgeable, collegial, and so on. The subjective modalities – multiple and different ways of being – I have described are quick examples of a never-ending list that directs teachers' pliable selves. However, the reduction of subjective modalities into easy-to-read list glosses over the importance of such a remark – this list represents a few of the ways teachers are deterritorialized.

I am struck not so much by the fact that educators are subject to so many explicit desires but by the implicit recognition that teachers are malleable, that they can *be* so many things. The laundry list of expectations for teachers pales in comparison to the assumption that teachers *be* in the first place. How might teachers be? To what extent are teachers implicated in their own being? What do teachers desire with regard to themselves? What do teachers experience about themselves?

The previous chapters described teachers' resistance to, and assemblage within, the performance accountability machine. This concluding chapter discusses the implications of the teacher subjectivities that were used in performance discourses that swirled around, and in, Delphi Elementary School. How might teachers consciously create themselves in relation to the enormous number of subjective modalities they encounter? How might teachers create themselves in relation to the different modalities documented in this research? In addition to exploring these questions, I explore potential modalities that did not arise in the case study data and raise the question: Did de-individualization contribute to a collective effulgence of resistance?

I discuss teachers' subjectivities in two ways: (1) as subjectival modalities – lines of flight – that attempted to deliberately thwart the surveillance of pedagogy and (2) as opportunities for micropolitical collective action, or opportunities for *subjective de-individualization*. However, an analysis of subjective transmogrifications, as discovered in the research, is predicated on a prior discussion about the ways in which a self, or subjectivity, can be used to form multiple identities that teachers might inhabit during their work. Readers should note, then, that the following discussion is the result of the research data. Bearing this in mind, Are teachers prepared to consciously inhabit their schizophrenic identities? Are teachers prepared to extend subjective modalities that were developed and used as "lines of flight, movements of deterritorialization and destratification" to resist accountability pressure (Deleuze & Guattari, 1987, p. 3)? Can experimental modalities of the teaching self form multiplicities of difference and, more importantly, groups of resistance? How?

HOW MIGHT TEACHERS BE? THE USES OF THE SELF

From the idea that the self is not given to us, I think that there is only one practical consequence: we have to create ourselves as a work of art.

– Foucault, "On the Geneaology of Ethics"

In the previous chapter, I described ways teachers created and used fabrications to refract the surveillance of pedagogy. These data are rich with meaning and implications. For instance, teachers created pedagogical fabrications intentionally and individually. Teachers discussed their concomitant schizophrenia as a result of performing these fabrications to different audiences. Teachers noted how, and in which ways, their *selves* were changing as an assemblage of accountability pressure, fabricated performances, and the swirling micropolitical pressure at Delphi. (It should be noted that some teachers were more aware of their transmogrifications than others.) The material effects of fabricating pedagogy produced different *beings,* beings that differed from those that existed when these educators began teaching. In the case of Julie, it could be said that she experienced the most noticeable deterritorialization as result of her lack of experience. The previous chapter mapped these cognitive transformations. And significant strategies for generating different ways of being at Delphi lay underneath these fabrications of practice. What regulated these performances?

Foucault (1980b, quoted and translated in Parras, 2006, p. 115) articulated a problem associated with "multiple identities": Is a self, or some form of consciousness, the regulator of subjective modalities?

Why, in what form, in a society like our own, does such a strong link exist between the exercise of power and the obligation for individuals to make of themselves, in procedures for the manifestation of truth . . . essential actors? What relation [exists] between the fact that one is a subject in a relation of power, and a subject by whom, for whom, and through whom the truth is manifest?

The idea of a self is important for two reasons. First, the idea offers the promise that policy does not dominate completely when teachers' practice is developed. However, policy was extremely powerful with regard to the ways teachers acted and behaved because teachers acted individually and did not realize how their fabrications were appropriated within Delphi. In this sense, accountability policy at Delphi acted as the ontological "strata" in which teachers performed their nomadic journeys. Second, the idea of a self or subjectivity offers the promise of new experimental opportunities for teachers to be – to "try out continuums of intensities" (Deleuze & Guattari, 1987, p. 161). In this second sense, the idea of the self observes experiments of subjective modalities.

If the implications of a malleable self are acknowledged, the focus shifts toward different modalities of the subjective and away from the policy environment. Of course, subjective transformations and policy disruptions need not be mutually exclusive. However, teachers in this study preferred – nearly unanimously – the production of different subjective modalities rather than collective action in response to state and district policy. Did teachers correctly estimate that they had little chance to rectify the poverty and alcohol abuse around Delphi? Did teachers correctly estimate their slim chances at reversing the accountability machine? Had teachers correctly estimated that collective action was impossible and that individual remakings of the self were the only pragmatic territory from which to traverse? Or were potential "external" political actions censored and hidden in some way from teachers? Finally, did teachers at Delphi enjoy developing and inhabiting their bifurcated identities? Was there micropolitical pleasure in the remaking of the self?

The promise of teacher power lies in the potential for new ways of being. This implication is derived directly from the data. Teachers in this research engaged in performances of pedagogy and multiple inhabitations of subjectivity rather than negotiating with policy-makers. Teachers knew they could succeed, to some extent, by inhabiting new nomadic and temporary identities – even if most of these new inhabitations were directed at colleagues. Teachers held a passport that allowed them to travel in this fragmented cognitive territory, and this passport allowed teachers to inhabit different nomadic identities at different times, in different registers, and within different knowledge, or discursive, practices (e.g., mathematics, reading, etc.). As a consequence, substantial research implications arose: What are the possible subjective modalities that teachers can produce? What is a "real" or "authentic" teacher, and what is a represented subjectivity of teaching? (Recall Magritte's declaration in the Preface: "This is not a pipe.") With what intentions will teachers explore nomadic experiments of the self? And finally, are nomadic journeys able to be grouped in some fashion (e.g., teaching tribes, non- or semi-sedentary nomadisms)?

Arts of Living and Pedagogical Suicide

The idea that teachers at Delphi fabricated identities, which contributed to professional schizophrenia, raised questions about who they were. Answers to questions about teacher identity could either be pursued through a study that searched for the essential, core, or true ingredients of educators at Delphi – which, of course, is what the war over teacher knowledge attempted. Or an answer to who teachers were at Delphi could be pursued through a study that attempted to understand questions of identity as differential products of subjectivity at different times, for different purposes, with different effects. Foucault (1990) discussed the grooming of the self as an "art of living." Foucault (1990) noted that the "arts of living" were a set of practices that were

> intentional and voluntary practices by which men not only fix rules of conduct for themselves, but seek to transform themselves, to modify themselves in their singular being, and to make of their life a work that bears certain aesthetic values and responds to certain criteria of style. (pp. 10-11)

In the Foucauldian sense, the notion of the self is not given, or predisposed; thus, the arts of living are not the means by which one unearths his or her own authenticity. Foucault's notion of the subjective is more plastic and malleable, more creative and aesthetic.

I included demographic data of all participants in Chapter 3. In doing so, I assumed that whatever inhabited identities participants had assumed prior to the study, however developed, would provide them with a nascent territory from which to embark on their nomadic experiments of the self. However, this descriptive data should not be read as anything like "core identities" but rather as the current and comfortable spaces from which they performed their work. The formation of subjectivities, then, was guided by aesthetics and style; it was not preordained. For instance, the crises of authenticity discussed in the previous chapter were the product of teachers feeling that they were betraying their core pedagogical beliefs, their core selves, in different ways. A different interpretation of these crises would be that teachers at Delphi were not prepared to travel on the nomadic journeys that re-articulated their selves. Understood this way, the perennial discourse about a "true self" permeated the thinking of participants and contributed directly to their feelings of professional guilt. Foucault (1983a), using Sartre as his familiar foil, commented:

> Through the moral notion of authenticity, [Sartre] turns back to the idea that we have to be ourselves – to be truly our true self. I think that the only acceptable practical consequence of what Sartre has said is to link his theoretical insight to the practice of creativity – and not of authenticity. From the idea that the self is not given to us, I think that there is only one practical

consequence: we have to create ourselves as a work of art . . . we should not have to refer the creative activity of somebody to the kind of relation he [*sic*] has to him [or her] self, but should relate the kind of relation one has to oneself to a creative activity. (p. 237)

The idea of the *aesthetic self* better explains teachers' multiple and conflicting identities at Delphi. In this sense, teachers were phronetic, doxa, epistemic, *and* mnemonic pedagogues, they were simultaneously temporary resistors and co-opted resistors, collegial allies and enemies, producers and consumers of images. Teachers were everything and, at times, nothing. However, experiments in subjective modalities require a word of caution.

I introduced this chapter with a quote from Deleuze and Guattari (1987) that describes the authors' understanding of how to transform the subjective or, in their terms, how to "make yourself a body without organs [BwO]." I believe that this particular quote resonates with the Foucauldian project of the subjective that I have described. However, the full Deleuze and Guattari (1987) quote includes a caveat, indeed a warning, in regard to experimenting with multiple subjectivities:

There are, in fact, several ways of botching the BwO: either one fails to produce it, or one produces it more or less, but nothing is produced on it, intensities do not pass or are blocked. This is because the BwO is always swinging between the surfaces that stratify it and the plane that sets it free. If you free it with too violent an action, if you blow apart the strata without taking precautions, then instead of drawing the plane you will be killed, plunged into a black hole, or even dragged toward catastrophe. Staying stratified – organized, signified, subjected – is not the worst that can happen; the worst that can happen is if you throw the strata into demented or suicidal collapse, which brings them back down on us heavier than ever. (p. 161)

The practice of experimenting with different subjectivities is precise, careful, and fateful work. The pedagogical nomads at Delphi often swung between different surfaces of accountability strata, providing glimpses into black holes of the self.

One important note about the arts of living is that they appear to be practiced individually – by the self. I will examine how teachers' subjective modalities acted as a "subject-group" within Delphi, assembling into micropolitical machines of phronetic desires (Deleuze & Guattari, 1983, p. 280). In this sense, did teachers' subjectivities form a micropolitical machine within Delphi? Were pedagogical fabrications and subjective effluences assembled in some fashion within the school? Returning to Chapter 2 for a moment, Smith (2005) asked:

If, as Deleuze and Guattari suggest, schizophrenia appears as the illness of our era, it is not as a function of generalities concerning our mode of life, but in relation to very precise [disciplinary] mechanisms of an economic, social and political nature. Our societies no longer function on the basis of codes and territorialities, but on the contrary on the basis of a massive decoding and deterritorialization. The schizophrenic is like the limit of our society, but a limit that is always avoided, reprimanded, abhorred. The problem of schizophrenia then becomes: how does one prevent the breakthrough from becoming a breakdown? How does one prevent the Body without Organs from closing in on itself, imbecilic and catatonic? How does one make the intense state triumph over the anguish, but without giving way to a chronic state, and even to a final state of generalized collapse, as is seen in the hospital? Is it possible to utilize the power of a lived chemistry and a schizo-logical analysis to ensure that the schizophrenic process does not turn into its opposite, that is, the production of the schizophrenic found in the asylum? If so, within what type of group, what kind of collectivity? (p. 190)

I later explore the ways that teachers' subjective modalities combined within various strata of the school. In this context, teachers' de-individualizations produced a different way of understanding political resistance or "organizing for action."

Pedagogical Desire, Micropolitical Pleasure, and the Schizophrenic Pedagogue

A particular problem that surfaced from this research is the extent to which teachers desired micropolitical activity (or perhaps more accurately, learned to desire micropolitical activity; that is, they acquired micropolitical pleasure). In the first chapter, I discussed the idea of "micropolitical pleasure" to characterize teachers' enjoyment of pedagogical problem solving. When this enjoyment was threatened or removed, teachers engaged in a number of micropolitical acts that attempted to retain control of pedagogical decision making and, hence, retain control of their desire. Why did teachers at Delphi perpetuate the circle of macropolitics   micropolitics? Why generate individual transmogrifications of the self instead of organizing for collective action? Clearly, fear of the accountability machine did not eliminate participants' micropolitics. In fact, in this research, the accountability machine shaped teachers' micropolitical actions in cases where they expressed the desire for more conformity to school norms. Was there something pleasurable about switching in and out of different subjective modalities? Did teachers enjoy their repression?

As is noted in Chapter 2, Deleuze and Guattari (1987) provide one answer to these kinds of questions:

Only microfascism provides an answer to the global question: Why does desire desire its own repression, how can it desire its own repression? The masses certainly do not passively submit to power; nor do they "want" to be repressed, in a kind of masochistic hysteria; nor are they tricked by an ideological lure ... It's too easy to be antifascist on the molar level, and not even see the fascist inside you, the fascist you yourself sustain and nourish and cherish with molecules both personal and collective. (p. 215)

If the idea of microfascism is applied to this case study, teachers' fabricated selves can be interpreted as cognitive battles within themselves. If teachers' political actions at Delphi were some form of democratic resistance to accountability fascism, then their multiple selves were the method that they used individually to traverse their microfascisms: macropolitics ↔ micropolitics. In this sense, Foucault's (1990) arts of living are intertwined in (micro)political struggles because the mutable self moves within different totalitarian and democratic spaces. Foucault (1983b) asked,

> How does one keep from being fascist, even (especially) when one believes oneself to be a revolutionary militant? How do we rid our speech and our acts, our hearts and our pleasures, of fascism? How do we ferret out the fascism that is ingrained in our behavior? The Christian moralists sought out the traces of the flesh lodged deep within the soul. Deleuze and Guattari, for their part, pursue the slightest traces of fascism in the body. (p. xiii)

If teachers and teacher educators desire the control of pedagogical decision making – which I believe they should – then it follows that they should be prepared, both macropolitically and micropolitically, for this phronetic knowledge contest. For instance, teacher preparation programs wrestle with the microfascisms of sexism and racism, particularly in relation to the diverse student populations teachers will encounter. While such practices are necessary in pre-service teacher education, they are insufficient when left to discussions of personal ethics. Teacher preparation programs must help teachers to confront the political work associated with these totalitarian impulses – as a set of macropolitics *and* as a set of micropolitics. Ethical discussions of microfascisms are necessary, but these discussions are insufficient if they do not invoke the political structures that shape teachers' selves – and within which teachers insert their multiple selves.

TEACHERS AS IMAGE MAKERS: A PEDAGOGICAL MICROPOLITICS OF MEANING

The preceding discussion about subjective modalities focused on the idea of the self as related to acts of teaching or to teachers as "being" rather than the more generic "subject," it was informed by evidence that teachers developed fabrications and inhabited new identities at Delphi, and it was directed purposefully toward the exploration of "internal" notions of the subjective – its possible existence, its affinity for identifying something as the "prediscursive" teacher, its potential for developing new micropolitical pedagogues, and so on.

I examine how subjective modalities could be exchanged in the open market of perceptions, impressions, and material rhetoric. To some extent, this is a return to Goffman's (1959, 1969) "presentations of the self" and "strategic interactions." However, I focus on the political exchanges encapsulated within teachers' selves. In this context, what are the micropolitics of subjectivity? What is the relationship, if any, between the sign and signified resistance to the surveillance of pedagogy that is accomplished through fabrications and different subjective modalities? Can subjective modalities be used as political currency within schools? Is the oasis of the authentic self simply a mirage perpetuated by accountability machines for continued consumption by teachers and schools?

CHAPTER 6

I discuss how pedagogical fabrications and situated subjectivites constituted teachers' politics within attempts to resist the surveillance of their practice. I sketch a *micropolitics of meaning* that formalizes the conscious application of pedagogical fabrications to thwart the surveillance of practice occurring in schools.

A Pedagogical Micropolitics of Meaning

Anderson (1991) noted that uses of impression management techniques were instances of "cognitive politics." Anderson (1991) raised the stakes of the accountability game when he suggested that teachers should increase their use of fabrications to manage the impressions of others. He stated, "If cognitive politics can be used for domination by those at the top, it can be used to promote counter-definitions of reality that reprofessionalize the teaching profession after years of de-skilling and standardization" (p. 137).

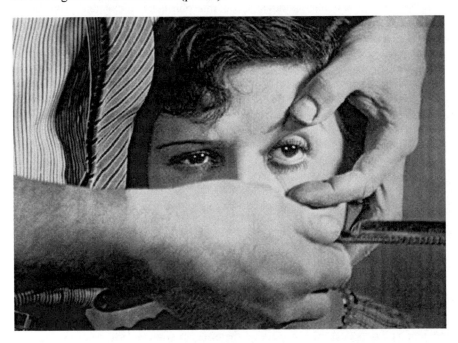

Figure 31. Luis Buñuel & Salvador Dalí. Un chien andalou. 1929. (Still image). © Salvador Dalí, Fundació Gala-Salvador Dalí / SODRAC (2008)

A micropolitics of meaning would provide teachers with a way to refract accountability demands that require visibility performances – akin to cutting the surveillant eye expressed by Luis Buñuel and Salvador Dalí above. At minimum, Anderson (1991) has suggested that preparation programs should introduce impression management techniques as a way to obfuscate accountability spectacles that sacrifice teachers and schooling for the economic and political gain of others. Such a call for teachers to deliberately fabricate performances will strike some readers as a disingenuous attempt at professionalization. What is really at stake is helping teachers to learn about the positivistic discourse of policy-makers and to appropriate this discourse in ways that complement their commitments. How is pre-service teacher education preparing educators for inevitable political conflicts over schooling?

If fabrications mark but one of many possible simulations, then fabrications need not be analyzed for their "authenticity," analyzed to the degree that they satisfy the accountability machine (which is circular – that is, it has already determined what is and is not authentic). Fabrications can be analyzed ontologically as one fabrication among a number of possible pedagogical simulations (Baudrillard, 1981). Consequently, teachers' fabrications could be understood for their political exegesis, or exchange value. Thus, teachers could reterritorialize the current performance discourse by speaking of effective and ineffective fabrications in relation to the democratic purposes of schooling, rather than simply meeting the demands of policy-makers and educational bureaucrats with "expected performance outcomes."

A micropolitics of meaning would invoke a form of educator resistance that is consistent with leadership theories about the social construction of meaning (Smirich & Morgan, 1982; Foster, 1989). A micropolitics of meaning may simply mean revisiting arguments about developing an educational technical language that may have no other purpose than to shape impressions about teachers' work in ways that privilege their situated knowledge in democratic ways (Mehan, 2001). Such a micropolitics of meaning is consistent with Anderson's (1991) cognitive politics and Lakoff's (2004) moral politics, and it is a concerted effort to (re)frame the discourse around educators' knowledge and epistemologies. Deleuze and Guattari's (1987) "micropolitics of perception, affection, [and] conversation" are examples of the micropolitical skills needed to resist disingenuous performance accountability systems (p. 208). If surveillance and other visibility technologies are able to co-opt teachers' knowledge, it is quite possible to reclaim teachers' subjective modalities for the pragmatic import of democracy. It remains to be seen if teachers, and teacher educators, are prepared for this political struggle.

DE-INDIVIDUALIZATION AND A MICROPOLITICS OF DIFFERENCE

Do not demand of politics that it restore the "rights" of the individual, as philosophy has defined them. The individual is the product of power. What is needed is to "de-individualize" by means of multiplication and displacement, diverse combinations. The group must not be the organic bond uniting hierarchized individuals, but a constant generator of de-individualization.

– Foucault, "Preface," Deleuze and Guattari, *Anti-Oedipus*

Here is a way of seeing the world: it is composed not of identities that form and reform themselves, but of swarms of difference that actualise themselves into specific forms of identity. Those swarms are not outside the world; they are not transcendent creators. They are of the world, as material as the identities formed from them. And they continue to exist even within the identities they form, not as identities but as difference. From their place within identities, these swarms of difference assure that the future will be open to novelty, to new identities and new relationships among them.

– Todd May, *Gilles Deleuze*

A persistent problem in this research was the fact that teachers practiced politics individually. Only rarely did teachers work together politically – although there is evidence that demonstrated that teachers worked together when trying to resolve logistical problems or pedagogical and curricular sequencing. However, these "collaborative" moments were not political responses to the accountability machine. In fact, the intensity of unequal power relations left teachers practicing politics alone. Fabrications, nomadic journeys, and subjective modalities were the political tools of the lonesome self. And, more importantly, teachers used these material rhetorics against each other, rather than combining them in some fashion for new practices and new formations of teaching selves. However, was it possible that teachers' fabricated selves acted in concert? Did these subjective emissions coalesce in some way within Delphi?

The idea that the self is mutable provides opportunities to think differently about teachers, teaching, and schooling. "Betrayal to oneself" was an idea that left teachers at Delphi isolated. Participants felt dishonest about some of their work when they created fabrications and inhabited new subjectivities (sometimes daily). In these cases, teachers entered new territories, willingly, but did so with feelings of shame. And, to compound the feelings of betrayal, teachers perpetuated distrust and paranoia among colleagues when they circulated fabrications for their peers to surveil. Deleuze and Guattari (1983) noted that

the paranoiac and the schizophrenic ... do not operate on the socius, but on the body without organs in a pure state. It might be said that the paranoiac ... makes us spectators to the imaginary birth of the mass phenomenon, and does so at a level that is still microscopic. (p. 281)

Multiplying Difference along Lines of Flight and Desires of Phronesis

Rather than arguing that individuals have fundamental and natural rights, we should perhaps try to imagine and create a new right of relations.

– Foucault, "The Social Triumph of the Sexual Will"

Fail to know what everyone else knows and you have a chance to create something interesting.

– Todd May, *Gilles Deleuze*

While participants shared democratic and fascist responses to the accountability machine, they did not combine their efforts consciously or intentionally. Teachers' nomadic subjectivities remained at the level of self-desires. However, multiplying difference as a way to de-individualize teachers is not about bringing educators into a collective or "community." In many ways, such an activity would reinforce power relations. There is simply too much empirical evidence about collegial activity in teaching that demonstrates how these communal attempts are locked in power relations that do not benefit educators (Hargreaves, 1991; Reed, 2000). Here, de-individualization is not about subordinating the self to a group but rather about multiplying the lines of flight and phronetic desires together in new rights of relations. Here, subjective modalities can be infinite, but the lines of resistance are direct.

Data from this research indicated that the teachers at Delphi were in fierce combat with the antidemocratic accountability machine. These contests were performed in the stratum of teachers' subjective differences. The constant struggle within this stratum was the pressure of power that fed teachers' feelings of betrayal, distrust, and paranoia within subjective performances. In this case, teachers' democratic lines of flight were tethered to striated notions of identity. And teachers felt guilty and ashamed whenever they deviated from *their given identities*. Subjective modalities were used to defend democratic teaching in relative isolation that fed into feelings of "identity betrayal." However, these fabrications and subjective modalities – while unstated to each other – formed a new machine within Delphi.

Rather than perpetuate feelings of betrayal, distrust, and paranoia that originate from ideas of a teacher identity, the possibilities of subjective modalities and desires of phronesis were multiplied and placed in new arrangements for "the creation of new forms of life, of relations, of friendships, in society, art, and culture" (Foucault, 1984a). And, of course, multiplying difference along lines of resistance was a micropolitical struggle. The "new" micropolitics of meaning sought subjective modalities and the multiplication of subjective differences that emanated from desires of phronesis. It did not seek solidarity of "identity." It swarmed, with different modalities, onto the fascism within accountability machines – a fascism that sought to extinguish teachers' phronesis. Deleuze and Guattari (1983) explained,

> It is therefore more a matter of the difference between two kinds of collections or populations: the large aggregates and the micromultiplicities. In both cases the investment is collective, it is an investment of a collective field ... Every investment is collective, every fantasy is a group fantasy and in this sense a position of reality. But the two kinds of investments are radically different ... One is a *subjugated group* investment, as much in its

sovereign form as in its colonial formations of the gregarious aggregate, which socially and psychically represses the desire of persons; the other, a *subject-group* investment in the transverse multiplicities that convey desire as a molecular phenomenon, that is, as partial objects and flows, as opposed to aggregates and persons. (p. 280)

Teachers acted as a subject group at Delphi. Their micropolitical actions were a molecular phenomenon that formed a machine within the school. Teachers were not alone, but they were made to feel lonely, isolated, and unaware of each other. "Every struggle is a function of all these undecidable propositions and constructs *revolutionary connections* in opposition to the *conjugations of the axiomatic*" (Deleuze & Guattari, 1987, p. 473).

Case Study Caveat

At this point, a likely question to ask of this research is the extent to which teachers at Delphi were "successful" with their micropolitics, with their "revolutionary connections" (Deleuze & Guattari, 1987, p. 473). However, the particular case study methodology that I used cannot provide an answer to such a question. This research was designed to identify phenomena and explain, to the best of my ability, the ways these phenomena operated. To answer questions of micropolitical success would require a different methodology, one designed to capture generalizations of place and person. This is not what this study set out to do. However, this study did identify teachers who acted as a subject group (borrowing from Deleuze & Guattari, 1987). Consequently, multiple case studies of this phenomenon could be developed to confirm such activity. And, from there, different designs could be developed to understand what effect, if any, teaching subject groups have on accountability machines.

THE NEW MICROPOLITICAL PEDAGOGUE

A micropolitics of meaning could seek ways to identify possible subjectivities through an experimentation of political self-expressions. Multiplying educator difference might seek ways to simultaneously de-individualize teachers while developing new cultural ways of educating and schooling that are based upon teachers' desire for phronesis. Teachers certainly do not need more and more people telling them what they are (which is often correlated to eliminating phronesis in their work). Teachers need to assert what they are, in relation to their desire for phronesis. A democratic teaching culture should stop defending itself; rather, such a culture should assert itself and creatively become teachers' desired knowledges. Teachers' nomadism seeks multiplicities of difference. Teacher nomads seek others. They seek to create and connect. This is how teachers survive.

Figure 32. Christopher John Lewis. Girl 1 and 2. 2000. Collection of Taylor Webb.

This is a teacher. It may not look like a teacher; it may not sound like a teacher; it may not behave like a teacher – but it is teacher.

Teachers: seek your difference. Perform your difference. Create your difference. And, if you feel safe, multiply your difference with other teaching nomads. Micropolitics, find your lines of flight, and teach through difference. Experiment. Help students find democratic alternatives. Destroy micro- and macro-instances of fascism. This is your power.

This is a teacher.

APPENDIX: INTERVIEW SCHEDULE

Introductory questions: Establishing teacher beliefs, desires, and enjoyment

1. Briefly review your academic background, including the schools that you attended and the degrees that you earned.
2. How long have you been teaching? How many years have you been in this district? School? Grade level?
3. Describe your current assignment (grade, subjects). What type of teaching structure do you work in (self-contained, open classroom, team, cluster, etc.)?
4. Why did you enter teaching? Are you still in teaching for the same reasons? Have your goals for teaching been fulfilled?
5. Are you satisfied with the amount of freedom (autonomy) that you have in your teaching? Why (Why not?)? In what ways does your freedom help your teaching? Does it impede your teaching? How?

Normative basis for micropolitics (and a description of that power)

7. Do you design your own lessons? Could you? Are you expected to? Is there a prescribed curriculum that you must follow?
8. Was there a time when teachers were split on an important curriculum issue? Why were they split? What happened?
9. What do teachers do when the faculty makes a curriculum decision they do not like (give an example)? How do they act? What do they do? (Repeat, substituting "faculty" with "district")
10. Do teachers ever just go along with a curriculum decision they don't support? Why? What do they do?
11. How do teachers lobby to teach something not included in the stated curriculum? Why do teachers lobby for ideas not included in stated curriculum? Whom do they consult?
12. How important is it to have consensus before teachers implement a new curricular or instructional decision? Why? How is consensus reached?
13. What can you do as an individual teacher to improve the education of students in this school?
14. What can teachers do collectively to improve the education of students in this school?

Surveillance and deterritorialization ↔ reterritorialization

15. How are standardized tests administered? How are the results used in the school? What impact do these tests have on your teaching?

16. Who *formally* supervises or evaluates your teaching? Could you describe how it works? Is it effective? Helpful?
17. Are there *informal* evaluations made of your teaching? By whom? In what ways?
18. Describe the impact of these [formal, then ask, informal] evaluations on your teaching? What do you do to prepare for these evaluations? Why?

Micropolitical spaces, geometries of influence

19. Where do most professional, as opposed to social, exchanges among teachers take place? What do teachers talk about in these exchanges?
20. Are you involved in any policy-making (union, curriculum, committee, principal's advisory committee, and district-wide committee)? Describe your role on the committee?
21. Describe the interaction between your principal and the faculty. Describe the impact your principal has on the school.
22. Describe the impact you have on your principal. Describe the impact you have on the school.
23. How has my presence in the school affected individuals or the school?

Territories/closing

23. Who really decides what is taught in your school? Why do they? How do they do it?
24. What does the term "politics" mean to you? "Power"? "Teacher politics"? "Teacher power"?

REFERENCES

Abelmann, C., & Elmore, R. (1999). *When accountability knocks, will anyone answer?* Philadelphia, PA: Consortium for Policy Research in Education (CPRE RR-42).

Achinstein, B., & Ogawa, R. T. (2006). (In) Fidelity: What the resistance of new teachers reveals about professional principles and prescriptive educational policies. *Harvard Educational Review, 76*(1), 30-63.

Airasian, P. W. (1988). Measurement driven instruction: A closer look. *Educational Measurement: Issues and Practice, 7*(4), 6-11.

Allen, A. (1999). Solidarity after identity politics: Hannah Arendt and the power of feminist theory. *Philosophy and Social Criticism, 25*(1), 97-118.

Anderson, G. (1991). Cognitive politics of principals and teachers: Ideological control in an elementary school. In J. Blase (Ed.), *The politics of life in schools: Power, conflict, and cooperation* (pp. 129-138). Newbury Park, CA: Sage.

Anyon, J. (1997). *Ghetto schooling: A political economy of urban educational reform.* New York: Teachers College Press.

Apple, M. W. (2001). *Educating the "right" way: Markets, standards, god and inequality.* New York: Routledge.

Apple, M. W. (2004). *Ideology and curriculum.* New York: Routledge.

Apple, M. W., Kenway, J., & Singh, M. (Eds.) (2005). *Globalizing education: Policies, pedagogies, & politics.* NY: Peter Lang.

Arendt, H. (1958). *The human condition.* Chicago: University of Chicago Press.

Aristotle (2002). *Nicomachean ethics.* Newburyport, MA: Focus.

Athanases, S. Z. & Achinstein, B. (2003) Focusing new teachers on individual and low performing students: The centrality of formative assessment in the mentor's repertoire of practice. *Teachers College Record, 105*(8), 1486-1520.

Ayers, W. (2004). *Teaching toward freedom: Moral commitment and ethical action in the classroom.* Boston: Beacon Press.

Bachrach, P., & Baratz, M. (1970). *Power and politics in organizations.* San Francisco, CA: Jossey-Bass.

Bacharach, S., & Mundell, B. (1993). Organizational politics in schools: Micro, macro, and the logics of action. *Educational Administration Quarterly, 29*(4), 423-452.

Baker, B. (2002). The hunt for disability: The new eugenics and the normalization of school children. *The Teachers College Record, 104*(4), 663-703.

Ball, D. L. (1990). Reflections and deflections of policy: The case of Carol Turner. *Educational Evaluation and Policy Analysis, 12*(3), 263-275.

Ball, S. J. (1997). Policy sociology and critical social research: A personal review of recent education policy and policy research. *British Educational Research Journal, 23*(3), 257-274.

Ball, S. J. (2001). Performativities and fabrication in the education economy: Towards the performative society. In D. Gleeson and C. Husbands (Eds.), *The performing school: Managing, teaching, and learning in a performance culture* (pp. 210-226). New York: Routledge.

Ball, S. J. (2003). The teacher's soul and the terrors of performativity. *Journal of Education Policy, 18*(2), 215-228.

Ball, S. J., & Bowe, R. (1991). Micropolitics of radical change: Budgets, management, and control in British schools. In J. Blase (Ed.), *The politics of life in schools: Power, conflict, and cooperation* (pp. 19-45). Newbury Park, CA: Sage.

Bassey, M. (1981). Pedagogic research: On the relative merits of the search for generalization and study of single events. *Oxford Review of Education, 7*(1), 73-93.

Baudrillard, J. (1981). *For a critique of the political economy of the sign.* St. Louis, MO: Telos Press.

Becker, H. (1990). Generalizing from case studies. In E. Eisner & A. Peshkin (Eds.), *Qualitative inquiry in education* (pp. 233-242). New York: Teachers College Press.

REFERENCES

Bell, J. (1999). *Doing your research project: A guide for first-time researchers in education and social science*. Philadelphia: Open University Press.

Biesta, G. (1995). Postmodernism and the repoliticization of education. *Interchange, 26*(2), 161-183.

Blase, J. (1987a). Political interactions among teachers: Sociocultural context in the school. *Urban Education, 22*(3), 286-309.

Blase, J. (1987b). The politics of teaching: The teacher-parent relationship and the dynamics of diplomacy. *Journal of Teacher Education, 38*(2), 53-60.

Blase, J. (1991). *The politics of life in schools: Power, conflict, and cooperation*. Thousand Oaks, CA: Corwin Press.

Blase, J., & Anderson, G. (1995). *The micropolitics of educational leadership: From control to empowerment*. New York: Teachers College Press.

Bolman, L., & Deal, T. (1991). *Reframing organizations: Artistry, choice and leadership*. San Francisco: Jossey-Bass.

Borko, H. (2004). Professional development and teacher learning: Mapping the terrain. *Educational Researcher, 33*(8), 3-15.

Bushnell, M. (2003). Teachers in the schoolhouse Panopticon: Complicity and resistance. *Education and Urban Society, 35*(3), 251-272.

Butler, J. (1990). *Gender trouble*. London: Routledge.

Carter, K. (1990). Teachers' knowledge and learning to teach. In W. R. Houston, M. Haberman, & J. Silkula (Eds.), *Handbook of research on teacher education* (pp. 291-310). New York: Macmillan.

Clandinin, D. J. (1992). Narrative and story in teacher education. In T. Russell and H. Munby (Eds.), *Teachers and teaching: From classroom to reflection* (pp. 124-137). Philadelphia: Falmer Press.

Clandinin, D. J., & Connelly, F. M. (1996). Teachers' professional knowledge landscapes: Teacher stories ... stories of teachers ... school stories ... stories of schools. *Educational Researcher, 19*(5), 2-14.

Clegg, S. (1989). *Frameworks of power*. Newbury Park, CA: Sage.

Cochran-Smith, M., & Fries, M. K. (2001). Sticks, stones, and ideology: The discourse of reform in teacher education. *Educational Researcher, 30*(8), 3-15.

Cochran-Smith, M., & Lytle, S. L. (1993). *Inside/outside: Teacher research and knowledge*. New York: Teachers College Press.

Cole, M. (2003). Might it be in the practice that it fails to succeed? A Marxist critique of claims for postmodernism and poststructuralism as forces for social change and social justice. *British Journal of Sociology of Education, 24*(4), 487-500.

Connelly, F. M., and Clandinin, D. J. (1990). Stories of experience and narrative inquiry. *Educational Researcher, 19*(5) 2-14.

Corbett, H. D. (1991). Community influence and school micropolitics: A case example. In J. Blase (Ed.), *The politics of life in schools: Power, conflict, and cooperation* (pp. 73-95). Thousand Oaks, CA: Corwin Press.

Coulter, D., & Wiens, J. R. (2002). Educational judgment: Linking the actor and the spectator. *Educational Researcher, 31*(4), 15-25.

Cuban, L. (1990). Reforming again, again, and again. *Educational Researcher, 19*(1), 3-13.

Curry, M., Jaxon, K., Russell, J. L., Callahan, M. A., & Bicais, J. (2008). Examining the practice of beginning teachers' micropolitical literacy within professional inquiry communities. *Teaching and Teacher Education, 24*(3), 660-673.

Dahl, R. (1961). *Who governs? Democracy and power in an American city*. New Haven, CT: Yale University Press.

Darling-Hammond, L. (2006). *Powerful teacher education: Lessons from exemplary programs*. San Francisco, CA: Jossey-Bass Publishers.

Darling-Hammond, L., & Sykes, G. (1999). *Teaching as the learning profession: Handbook of policy and practice*. San Francisco, CA: Jossey-Bass Publishers.

Deleuze, G. (1992). Postscript on the societies of control. *October, 59*, 3-7.

Deleuze, G., & Guattari, F. (1983). *Anti-Oedipus: Capitalism and schizophrenia.* (R. Hurley, M. Seem, & H. R. Lane, Trans.). Minneapolis: University of Minnesota Press.

Deleuze, G., & Guattari, F. (1987). *A thousand plateaus: Capitalism and schizophrenia.* Minneapolis, MN: University of Minnesota.

De Lissovoy, N., & McLaren, P. (2003). Educational "accountability" and the violence of capital: A Marxian reading. *Journal of Educational Policy, 18*(2), 131-143.

Diorio, J. A. (1982). Knowledge, autonomy, and the practice of teaching. *Curriculum Inquiry, 12*(3), 257-282.

Dreyfus, H., & Rabinow, P. (1982). *Michel Foucault: Beyond structuralism and hermeneutics.* Chicago: The University of Chicago Press.

Dumas, M. J., & Anyon, J. (2006). *Toward a critical approach to educational policy implementation: Implications for the (battle) field.* Albany, NY: State University Press.

Earl, L. M. (1999). Assessment and accountability in education: Improvement or surveillance? *Education Canada, 39*(3), 4-6, 47.

Elbaz, F. (1981). The teacher's "practical knowledge": Report of a case study. *Curriculum Inquiry, 11*(1), 43-71.

Elbaz, F., and Elbaz, R. (1983). Knowledge, discourse, and practice: A response to Diorio's "knowledge, autonomy and the practice of teaching." *Curriculum Inquiry, 13*(2), 151-156.

Elmore, R. (2005). Accountable leadership. *The Educational Forum, 69*(2), 134-142.

Elmore, R., & Sykes, G. (1992). Curriculum policy. In P. Jackson (Ed.), *Handbook of research on curriculum* (pp. 155-215). New York: MacMillan.

Emerson, R., Fretz, R., & Shaw, L. (1995). *Writing ethnographic fieldnotes.* Chicago: University of Chicago Press.

Erickson, F. (1986). Qualitative methods in research on teaching. In M. C. Wittrock (Ed.), *Handbook of research on teaching* (pp. 119-161). New York: MacMillan.

Fendler, L. (2003). Teacher reflection in a hall of mirrors: Historical influences and political reverberations. *Educational Researcher, 32*(3), 16-25.

Fenstermacher, G. D., & Amarel, M. (1983). The interests of the student, the state, and humanity in education. In L. Shulman & G. Sykes (Eds.), *The handbook on teaching and policy* (pp. 392-407). New York: Longman.

Feuer, M. J., Towne, L., & Shavelson, R. J. (2002). Scientific culture and educational research. *Educational Researcher, 31*(8), 4-14.

Finn, C. E., & Wilcox, D. D. (2000, January 13). Teachers should be graded on how well their students are learning. *Los Angeles Times*, p. B9.

Foster, W. (1989). Toward a critical practice of leadership. In J. Smyth (Ed.), *Critical perspectives on educational leadership* (pp. 39-62). New York: The Falmer Press.

Foucault, M. (1970). *The order of things: An archaeology of human sciences.* New York: Random House.

Foucault, M. (1972). *The archaeology of knowledge and the discourse on language.* New York: Random House.

Foucault, M. (1977). *Discipline and punish: The birth of the prison.* New York: Vintage/Random House.

Foucault, M. (1980a). *Du gouvernement des vivants.* (Audio recording.) Paris: Bibliothèque Générale du Collège de France.

Foucault, M. (1980b). *Power/knowledge: Selected interviews and other writings.* New York: Pantheon.

Foucault, M. (1981). *Subjectivité et vérité* (audio recording). Paris: Bibliothèque Générale du Collège de France.

Foucault, M. (1982a). The subject and power. In H. Dreyfus & P. Rabinow (Eds.), *Michel Foucault: Beyond structuralism and hermeneutics* (pp. 208-226). Chicago: The University of Chicago Press.

Foucault, M. (1982b). The social triumph of the sexual will: A conversation with Michel Foucault (G. Barbedette, Interviewer, B. Lemon, Trans.). *Christopher Street, 6*(4), 36-41.

REFERENCES

Foucault, M. (1983a). On the genealogy of ethics: An overview of work in progress. In H. Dreyfus & P. Rabinow (Eds.), *Michel Foucault: Beyond structuralism and hermeneutics* (pp. 229-252). Chicago: The University of Chicago Press.

Foucault, M. (1983b). Preface. In G. Deleuze and F. Guattari, *Anti-Oedipus: Capitalism and schizophrenia* (pp. xi-xiv). Minneapolis: University of Minnesota Press.

Foucault, M. (1983c). *This is not a pipe: Illustrations and letters by René Magritte* (J. Harkness, Trans.; R. Magritte, Illus.). Berkeley: University of California Press.

Foucault, M. (1984a). *The Foucault reader* (Ed. P. Rabinow). New York: Pantheon.

Foucault, M. (1984b). Michel Foucault, an interview: Sex, power, and the politics of identity (B. Gallagher and A. Wilson, Interviewers). *The Advocate 400*(58), 26-30, 58.

Foucault, M. (1990). *The history of sexuality: The Use of Pleasure, Vol. 2*. New York: Vintage.

Fraser, N. (1989). *Unruly practices: Power, discourse, and gender in contemporary social theory*. Minneapolis: University of Minnesota Press.

Freire, P. (1998). *Teachers as cultural workers: Letters to those who dare teach*. Boulder, CO: Westview.

French, J., & Raven, B. (1959). The bases of social power. In D. Cartwright (Ed.). *Studies in social power* (pp. 150-167). Ann Arbor: University of Michigan Press.

Fuhrman, S. H. (1999). *The new accountability*. CPRE Policy Brief No. RB-27. Philadelphia, PA: University of Pennsylvania/Consortium for Policy Research in Education.

Gale, T. (2001). Critical policy sociology: Historiography, archaeology and genealogy as methods of policy analysis. *Journal of Education Policy, 16*(5), 379-393.

Geertz, C. (1973). *The interpretation of cultures*. New York: Basic Books.

Giddens, A. (1984). *The constitution of society: Outline of the theory of structuration*. Berkeley: University of California Press.

Gleeson, D., & Husbands, C. (2003). Modernizing schooling through performance management: A critical appraisal. *Journal of Education Policy, 18*(5), 499-511.

Glesne, C. (1999). *Becoming qualitative researchers: An introduction*. New York: Longman.

Goffman, E. (1959). *The presentation of self in everyday life*. New York: Doubleday.

Goffman, E. (1969). *Strategic interaction*. Philadelphia: University of Pennsylvania Press.

Goodlad, J. (1975). *The dynamics of educational change: Toward responsive schools*. New York: McGraw-Hill.

Goodwin, C., & Duranti, A. (1992). Rethinking context: An introduction. In A. Duranti & C. Goodwin (Eds.), *Rethinking context: Language as an interactive phenomenon* (pp. 1-42). New York: Cambridge University Press.

Greenfield, W. (1991). The micropolitics of leadership in an urban elementary school. In J. Blase (Ed.), *The politics of life in schools: Power, conflict, and cooperation* (pp. 161-184). Newbury Park: CA, Sage.

Grossman, P. L. (1989). A study in contrast: Sources of pedagogical content knowledge for secondary English. *Journal of Teacher Education, 40*(5), 24-31.

Grossman, P. L., & Thompson, C. (2004). District policy and beginning teachers: A lens on teacher learning. *Educational Evaluation and Policy Analysis, 26*(4), 281-301.

Gulson, K. (2006). A white veneer: Education policy, space and race in the inner city. *Discourse: Studies in the Cultural Politics of Education, 27*(2), 259-274.

Gutmann, A. (1999). *Democratic education*. Princeton, NJ: Princeton University Press

Haggerty, K. D., & Ericson, R. V. (2000). The surveillant assemblage. *British Journal of Sociology, 51*(4), 605-622.

Hargreaves, A. (1991). Contrived collegiality: The micropolitics of teacher collaboration. In J. Blase (Ed.), *The politics of life in schools: Power, conflict, and cooperation* (pp. 46-72). Thousand Oaks: CA: Corwin Press.

Hargreaves, A. (1996). Transforming knowledge: Blurring the boundaries between research, policy, and practice. *Educational Evaluation and Policy Analysis, 18*(2), 105-122.

Hargreaves, A. (2003). *Teaching in the knowledge society: Education in the age of insecurity*. New York: Teachers College Press.

Hartsock, N. C. M. (1983). *Money, sex, and power: Toward a feminist historical materialism*. New York: Longman.

Hiebert, J., Gallimore, R., & Stigler, J. W. (2002). A knowledge base for the teaching profession: What would it look like and how can we get one? *Educational Researcher, 31*(5), 3-15.

Hobbes, T. (1660/1982). *Leviathan*. New York: Penguin Classics.

Honig, M. I. (2006). *New directions in education policy implementation: Confronting complexity*. New York: State University of New York.

Hyland, N. E. (2005). Being a good teacher of black students? White teachers and unintentional racism. *Curriculum Inquiry, 35*(4), 429-459.

Ingersoll, R. M. (2003). *Who controls teachers' work? Power and accountability in America's schools*. Cambridge, MA: Harvard University Press.

Ingersoll, R. M., & Smith, T. M. (2003). The wrong solution to the teacher shortage. *Educational Leadership, 60*(8), 30-33.

Jeffrey, B. (2002). Performativity and primary teacher relations. *Journal of Education Policy, 17*(5), 531-546.

Johnson, B. (2004). Local school micropolitical agency: An antidote to new managerialism. *School Leadership and Management, 24*(3), 267-286.

Johnson, B. L. (2001). Micropolitical dynamics of educational interests: A view from within. *Educational Policy, 15*(1), 115-134.

Jones, E. E., and Pitman, T. S. (1982) Toward a general theory of strategic self-presentation. In J. Suls (Ed.), *Psychological perspectives on the self (Vol. 1)* (pp. 231-262). Hillsdale, NJ: Erlbaum.

Kelchtermans, G. (2007). Macropolitics caught up in micropolitics: The case of the policy on quality in Flanders (Belgium). *Journal of Education Policy, 22*(4), 471-491.

Kelchtermans, G., & Ballet, K. (2002). The micropolitics of teacher inductio: A narrative-biographical study on teacher socialisation. *Teaching and Teacher Education, 18*(1), 105-120.

Kelly, D. M. (2003). Practicing democracy in the margins of school: The teenage parents program as feminist counterpublic. *American Educational Research Journal, 40*(1), 123-146.

Kennedy, M. M. (1999). Approximations to indicators of student outcomes. *Educational Evaluation and Policy Analysis, 21*(4), 345-363.

Korthagen, F. A., & Kessels, J. P. (1999). Linking theory and practice: Changing the pedagogy of teacher education. *Educational Researcher, 28*(4), 4-17.

Kozol, J. (2005). The shame of the nation: The restoration of apartheid schooling in America. New York: Crown Publishers.

Lakoff, G. (2004). Don't think of an elephant: Know your values and frame the debate. White River Junction, VT: Chelsea Green Publishing Company.

Little, J. W. (1989). District policy choices and teachers' professional development opportunities. *Educational Evaluation and Policy Analysis, 11*(2), 165-179.

Loeb, P. S. (2007). Suicide, meaning, and redemption. In M. Dries (Ed.), *Nietzsche on time and history*. Berlin: Walter de Gruyter Press.

Lortie, D. C. (1975). *Schoolteacher: A sociological study*. Chicago: University of Chicago Press.

Loucks-Horsley, S., Hewson, P., Love, N., & Stiles, K. (1998). *Designing professional development for teachers of science and mathematics*. Thousand Oaks, CA: Corwin Press.

Lukes, S. (1974). *Power: A radical view*. London: The MacMillan Press.

Lukes, S. (1977). *Essays in social theory*. New York: Columbia University Press.

Lyotard, J. F. (1984). *The postmodern condition: A report on knowledge*. Minneapolis: University of Minnesota Press.

MacDonald, H. (1998, July 20). The flaw in student-centered learning. *The New York Times*.

MacGillivray, L., Ardell, A. L., Curwen, M. S., & Palma, J. (2004). Colonized teachers: Examining the implementation of a scripted reading program. *Teaching Education, 15*(2), 131-144.

Machiavelli, N. (1513/1981). *The prince*. New York: Penguin Books.

REFERENCES

Madison, D. S. (2005). *Critical ethnography: Method, ethics, and performance*. Thousand Oaks, CA: Sage.

Malen, B. (2001). Generating interest in interest groups. *Educational Policy, 15*(1), 168-186.

Malen, B., & Knapp, M. (1997). Rethinking the multiple perspectives approach to education policy analysis: Implications for policy-practice connections. *Journal of Education Policy, 12*(5), 419-445.

Malen, B., & Ogawa, R. (1988). Professional-patron influence on site-based governance councils: A confounding case study. *Educational Evaluation and Policy Analysis, 10*(4), 251-270.

Marceau, J. (1993). *Steering from a distance: International trends in the financing and governance of higher education*. Canberra, ACT: Australian Government Publishing Service.

Massey, D. (1994). *Space, place, and gender*. Minneapolis: University of Minnesota Press.

Mawhinney, H. B. (1999). Reappraisal: The problems and prospects of studying the micro-politics of leadership in reforming schools. *School Leadership and Management, 19*(2), 159-170.

Maxcy, S. J. (1991). *Educational leadership: A critical pragmatic perspective*. New York: Bergin and Garvey.

May, T. (2005). *Gilles Deleuze: An introduction*. New York: Cambridge University Press.

May, T. (2007). Jacques Rancière and the ethics of equality. *SubStance: A Review of Theory and Literary Criticism, 36*(2), 20-36.

McCracken, G. (1988). *The long interview*. Newbury Park, CA: Sage.

McDonald, J. P., & Klein, E. J. (2003). Networking for teacher learning: Toward a theory of effective design. *Teachers College Record, 105*(8), 1606-1621.

McGivney, J. H., & Haught, J. M. (1972). The politics of education: A view from the perspective of the central office staff. *Educational Administration Quarterly, 8*(3), 18-38.

McLaughlin, M. W. (1987). Learning From experience: Lessons from policy implementation. *Educational Evaluation and Policy Analysis, 9*(2), 171-178.

McNeil, L. (2000). *Contradictions of school reform: Educational costs of standardized testing*. New York: Routledge.

Mehan, H. (2001). The construction of an LD student: A case study in the politics of representation. In S. Taylor, S. Yates, & M. Wetherell (Eds.), *Discourse Theory and Practice* (pp. 345-363). Thousand Oaks, CA: Sage.

Moore-Johnson, S. (1990). Teachers at work: Achieving success in our schools. NY: Basic Books.

Newmann, F., King, M. B., & Rigdon, M. (1997). Accountability and school performance. *Harvard Educational Review, 67*(1), 41-69.

Nietzsche, F. (1968). *The will to power*. (W. Kaufman, Ed., R. J. Hollingdale, Trans.). New York: Vintage.

Noblit, G., Berry, B., & Dempsey, V. (1991). Political responses to reform: A comparative case study. *Education and Urban Society, 23*(4), 379-395.

Noddings, N. (1986). Fidelity in teaching, teacher education, and research for teaching. *Harvard Educational Review, 56*(4), 496-510.

Oakes, J., & Lipton, M. (2006). *Teaching to change the world*. New York: McGraw-Hill.

O'Day, J. (2002). Complexity, accountability, and school improvement. *Harvard Educational Review, 72*(3), 293-329.

Odden, A., & Kelley, C. (2002). *Paying teachers for what they know and do: New and smarter compensation strategies to improve schools*. Newbury Park, CA: Sage.

OECD. (2007). *Education at a glance 2007:* OECD indicators complete edition-ISBN 9264032878. *Source OECD Education & Skills, 2007*, 1-449.

Olssen, M., Codd, J. A., & O'Neill, A. M. (2004). *Education policy: Globalization, citizenship, and democracy*. Thousand Oaks, CA: Sage.

Parras, E. (2006). *Foucault 2.0*. New York: Other Press.

Patterson, J. A., & Marshall, C. (2001). Making sense of policy paradoxes: A case study of teacher leadership. *Journal of School Leadership, 11*(5), 372-398.

Pearson, P. D. (2004). The reading wars. *Educational Policy, 18*(1), 216-252.

Peters, M. (2003). Post-structuralism and Marxism: Education as knowledge capitalism. *Journal of Education Policy, 18*(2), 115-129.

Pfeffer, J. (1981). *Power in organizations*. Marshfield, MA: Pitman.

Pignatelli, F. (2002). Mapping the terrain of a Foucauldian ethics: A response to the surveillance of schooling. *Studies in Philosophy and Education, 21*(2), 157-180.

Pinar, W., Reynolds, W. M., Slattery, P., & Taubman, P. M. (1995). *Understanding curriculum.* New York: Peter Lang.

Portin, B. (1995). Primary headship in a time of systemic change: Conceptions of leadership. Unpublished doctoral dissertation, Oxford University, England.

Psacharopoulos, G., & Patrinos, H. A. (2004). Returns to investment in education: A further update. *Education Economics,* 12 (2), 111-134.

Putnam, R. T., & Borko, H. (2000). What do new views of knowledge and thinking have to say about research on teacher learning? *Educational Researcher, 29*(1), 4-15.

Ransom, J. S. (1997). *Foucault's discipline: The politics of subjectivity.* Durham, NC: Duke University Press.

Reed, C. J. (2000). *Teaching with power: Shared decision-making and classroom practice.* New York: Teachers College Press.

Reyes, P., & Rorrer, A. (2001). US school reform policy, state accountability systems and the limited English proficient student. *Journal of Education Policy, 16*(2), 163-178.

Sachs, J. (2001). Teacher professional identity: Competing discourses, competing outcomes. *Journal of Education Policy, 16*(2), 149-161.

Sarason, S. (1982). *The culture of the school and the problem of change.* Boston: Allyn and Bacon.

Scheurich, J. J. (1994). Policy archaeology: A new policy studies methodology. *Journal of Education Policy, 9*(4), 297-316.

Schoenfeld, A. H. (2004). The math wars. *Educational Policy, 18*(1), 253-286.

Schwille, J., Porter, A., Belli, G., Floden, R., Freeman, D., Knappen, L., & Kuhs, T. (1986). Teachers as policy brokers in the context of elementary school mathematics. In L. Shulman & G. Sykes (Eds.), *The handbook on teaching and policy* (pp. 370-391). New York: Longman.

Scott, J. C. (1990). *Domination and the arts of resistance: Hidden transcripts.* New Haven, CT: Yale University Press.

Segall, A. (2004). Revisiting pedagogical content knowledge: The pedagogy of content/the content of pedagogy. *Teaching and Teacher Education, 20*(5), 489-504.

Shore, C., & Wright, S. (2004). Whose accountability? Governmentality and the auditing of universities. *Parallax, 10*(2), 100-116.

Shulman, L. (1997). Disciplines of inquiry in education: A new overview. In R. Jaeger (Ed.), *Complimentary methods for research in education* (pp. 3-29). Washington, DC: American Educational Research Association.

Shulman, L. S. (1986). Those who understand: Knowledge growth in teaching. *Educational Researcher, 15*(2), 4-14.

Sibeon, R. (2004). *Rethinking social theory.* Thousand Oaks, CA: Sage.

Silverman, D. (Ed.) (2004). *Qualitative research: Theory, method and practice* (2nd ed.). Thousand Oaks, CA: Sage.

Sirotnik, K. A. (1989). The school as the center of change. In T. J. Sergiovanni & J. H. Moore (Eds.). *Schooling for tomorrow: Directing reforms to issues that count* (pp. 89-113). Newton, MA: Allyn and Bacon.

Sirotnik, K. A. (2004). *Holding accountability accountable: What ought to matter in public education.* New York: Teachers College Press.

Sirotnik, K. A., & Kimball, K. (1999). Standards for standards-based accountability systems. *Phi Delta Kappan, 81*(3), 209-214.

Smirich, L., & Morgan, G. (1982). Leadership: The management of meaning. *Journal of Applied Behavioral Science, 18*(3), 257-273.

REFERENCES

Smith, D. (2005). Critical, clinical. In C. Stivale (Ed.), *Gilles Deleuze: Key concepts* (pp. 182-193). Montreal, QC, and Kingston, ON: McGill-Queen's University Press.

Smith, M. L., & Miller-Kahn, L. (2003). *Political spectacle and the fate of American schools.* New York: Falmer Press.

Smyth, J. (2002). Unmasking teachers' subjectivities in local school management. *Journal of Education Policy, 17*(4), 463-482.

Solomon, R. P. (2002). School leaders and antiracism: Overcoming pedagogical and political obstacles. *Journal of School Leadership, 12*(2), 174-197.

Spillane, J. P., Diamond, J. B., Burch, P., Hallett, T., Jita, L., & Zoltners, J. (2002). Managing in the middle: School leaders and the enactment of accountability Policy. *Educational Policy, 16*(5), 731-762.

Stanley, J., & Steinhardt, B. (2003) *Bigger monster, weaker chains: The growth of an American surveillance society.* Retrieved from http://www.aclu.org/Privacy/Privacy.cfm?ID=11573&c=39.

Stitch, S. (1990). *Anxious visions: Surrealist art.* New York: Abbeville Press/Regents of California, Berkeley.

Supovitz, J. A. (2002). Developing communities of instructional practice. *Teachers College Record, 104*(8), 1591-1626.

Talbert, J., McLaughlin, M., & Rowan, B. (1993). Understanding context effects on secondary school teaching. *Teachers College Record, 95*(1), 45-68.

Timperley, H., & Alton-Lee, A. (2008). Reframing teacher professional learning: An alternative policy approach to strengthening valued outcomes for diverse learners. *Review of Research in Education, 32*(1), 328.

Toll, C. (2002). Can teachers and policy makers learn to talk to one another? *The Reading Teacher, 55*(4), 318-325.

Tom, A. R. (1983). Practice is more than a technical activity: A response to Diorio's "knowledge, autonomy and the practice of teaching." *Curriculum Inquiry, 13*(2), 157-163.

Turnley, W., & Bolino, M. (2001). Achieving desired images while avoiding undesired images: Exploring the role of self-monitoring in impression management. *Journal of Applied Psychology, 86*(2), 351-360.

Tyack, D. (1974). *The one best system: A history of American urban education.* Cambridge: Harvard University Press.

Vidovich, L. (2007). Removing policy from its pedestal: Some theoretical framings and practical possibilities. *Educational Review, 59*(3), 285-298.

Vygotsky, L. S. (1962). *Language and thought.* Cambridge, MA: MIT Press.

Warren, D. I. (1968). Power, visibility, and conformity in formal organizations. *American Sociological Review, 33*, 951-971.

Webb, P. T. (2001). Reflection and reflective teaching: Ways to improve pedagogy or ways to remain racist? *Race, Ethnicity and Education, 4*(3), 245-252.

Weick, K. E. (1976). Educational organizations as loosely coupled systems. *Administrative Science Quarterly, 21*(1), 1-19.

Whitford, B. L., & Jones, K. (2000). *Accountability, assessment, and teacher commitment: Lessons from Kentucky's reform efforts.* Albany, NY: State University of New York Press.

Whitty, G. (2006). Education(al) research and education policy making: Is conflict inevitable? *British Educational Research Journal, 32*(2), 159-176.

Wilcox, D, & Finn, C. (1999). Board games: Failure of the National Board for Professional Teaching Standards to accomplish objective of improving quality of teaching in the US; Business backs a losing education strategy. *National Review, 51*(15), 26-27.

Wilson, S., & Wineburg, S. (1993). Wrinkles in time and place: Using performance assessments to understand the knowledge of history teachers. *American Educational Research Journal, 30*(4), 729-769.

Wirt, F., & Kirst, M. (1997). *The political dynamics of American education.* Berkeley, CA: McCutchan Publishing Corporation.

Witherspoon, P. D. (1997). *Communicating leadership: An organizational approach.* Boston: Allyn and Bacon.

Wolcott, H. (1997). Ethnographic research in education. In R. Jaeger (Ed.), *Complimentary methods for research in education* (pp. 327-353). Washington, DC: American Educational Research Association.

Wong, K. K. (1999). *Funding public schools: Politics and policies.* Lawrence: University Press of Kansas.

Woods, P., & Jeffrey, B. (2002). The reconstruction of primary teachers' identities. *British Journal of Sociology of Education, 23*(1), 89-106.

Yin, R. (1989). *Case study research: Design and methods.* London: Sage.

Youdell, D. (2006). Diversity, inequality, and a post-structural politics for education. *Discourse: Studies in the Cultural Politics of Education, 27*(1), 33-42.

Zakaria, F. (1997). The rise of illiberal democracy. *Foreign Affairs, 76*(6), 22-43.

Zembylas, M. (2003). Interrogating "teacher identity." *Educational Theory, 53*(1), 107-127.

Zembylas, M. (2007). Risks and pleasures: A Deleuzo-Guattarian pedagogy of desire in education. *British Educational Research Journal, 33*(3), 331-347.

LaVergne, TN USA
13 December 2010

208598LV00002B/1/P